INCARNATING GRACE

REFLECTING THE GLORY OF JESUS' GRACE THROUGH A CLOSER WALK WITH HIM

DOYLE WALSTROM

AMAZON

Scripture taken from THE HOLY BIBLE, NEW INTERNATIONAL VERSION ®.
Copyright©
1973, 1978, 1984, 2011 by Biblica, Inc.™. Used by permission of Zondervan.

Cover image: iStock – Title 157603393 – Teton Range, Grand Teton

ISBN – 978-0-578-93140-1

Continue the discussion at:
incarnatinggrace.org
or
find me on Facebook

This book is dedicated to Heather and Ben who patiently endured my absence while writing it and encouraged me all along the way. I love you guys beyond words.

ACKNOWLEDGEMENT

My thanks to Laura Lundgren who not only labored hard at editing but also pushed me to instill true life into these pages. Thanks, too, to my friend, Charles (Chuck) Anderson, and to my bride, Heather, for a very thorough proof-read and great advice and suggestions to help me through the rougher parts of my writing.

Finally, a special thanks to my friend, Michael Card, for his very gracious foreword to the book.

CONTENTS

FOREWORD

By Michael Card

When we come to the subject of grace, the first question must always be, "What did Jesus say about grace?" The answer is, in the Gospels He does not speak the word at all. (That is the Greek word "charis.") Indeed, in 2 Corinthians 12:9, He tells Paul that his charis is sufficient for him, but in the Gospels not a word. In John's monumental introduction to his Gospel, he tells us twice that Jesus is full of "charis and truth" (1:14,17) echoing God's revelation of Himself to Moses in Exodus 34. So, Jesus' grace is sufficient and He is full of grace, yet He never uses the word nor gives an explanation.

This is not to say that grace does not make it into His teaching, primarily the parables. You might say that there is an element of grace in practically all of the parables. The rich man pays the laborers who have worked an hour the same as he does those who have "born the heat of the day." The Samaritan, the last person we would have expected to see grace exhibited from, lavishes it on the wounded man by the side of the road. And perhaps greatest of all, the father of the prodigal son, shows remarkable charis to a son who has all but spit in his face. While Jesus may not say the word "grace," He paints numerous pictures of it in His parables.

What is most significant is the way Jesus incarnates grace. He lives it and exudes it in all of His various interactions. The disciples repeatedly tell Him that this or that person is not worthy of His attention. Yet Jesus always makes time (i.e., shows grace) to the lame and the leper and the children who are considered unworthy. To someone like Matthew, an outcast, Jesus extends the invitation to become a principal follower. He accepts as His principal supporters a group of women who would have been considered "second class citizens." Jesus exhibits an element of grace in everything He does.

So now it's down to us. How do we respond to His extravagant example? We delve into the Scriptures and listen to what they say about the grace of God. We gather together as many thoughts as we can from Paul, Peter and the others who knew Jesus. Thankfully, Doyle Walstrom has started this homework for us. HE has listened to the text of Scripture and written a book not just to help us understand "charis" but to encourage us to begin incarnating it the way Jesus did.

INTRODUCTION

Have you ever been faced with the impossible? I'm not talking about the difficult, that's a different story. All of us need to deal with the difficult every day. I'm talking about a task where there is no hope whatsoever of success. For me, the impossible has been the pursuit of living a successful Christian life. As hard as I tried, I never could seem to live in a way that made me feel as though I was living the way I should. I always felt as though I was falling short of what a Christian should be, how a true Christian should live. I think I have a lot of company in this regard.

Even as a young boy, I struggled with a furious temper that led to so many difficulties in my life and right on into my marriage. It was one of the first truly difficult challenges my wife, Heather, and I had to work through. There were a lot of frustrations in my family history that led up to this. I grew up in a home without a father. He died in a job-related accident when I was one year old, leaving behind a wife and six children ranging from ages one to thirteen. At the time, no one in the family knew Christ and we were left with a lot of frustration and pain, especially for my mom and older siblings who felt his loss most deeply. A culture of anger arose in our family as we struggled with our grief and our questions.

Being a Christian seemed easy at first. As a new believer, even though I was young, I realized that I had been forgiven of my sin and guilt which produced a lot of joy in me. I sensed a peace with God. However, that was about the time it started - the impossible began to settle in.

As Christians, we desire to live holy lives and to live righteously before God. It is something that is instilled into us by the Holy Spirit (1 Peter 1:2). This is reinforced by those who teach God's word. We understand that we have been separated from the world and are no longer to live for the things of the world. On top of all this, Charles Stanley has said that God's will for our lives is found in Romans 8:29, that we are to be "conformed to the image of his Son." We are to resemble Jesus in his character and conduct. That, he says, is the true meaning of a life of holiness, or sanctification.[1] No pressure there, right?

God's standard of holiness begins to seem more and more impossible. I noticed that my excitement for God cooled from when I was first saved. It became harder not only to control my temper, but many other sins began to surface as well. Not long after I accepted Christ into my life, my mom remarried and the relationship I had with my stepfather was rocky at best. I was faced with the impossible task of getting along with parents that I had chosen not to respect.

All of this led to a painful disconnect in my life between who I wanted to be and who I really was. I remember reading impossible-sounding commands like 1 Peter 1:15-16, which says, "But just as He who called you is holy, so be holy in all you do; for it is written: "Be holy, because I am holy." I wanted to be good and to do good, but my experience was something entirely different. I knew who I was when no one was looking. As hard as I tried, I was not living a holy life. I knew that I was faced with an impossible task and felt my failure every time I sinned. For a time, I even walked away from my relationship with Jesus.

So, where does this conflict come from? Why are we faced with this impossible task of the Christian life? It all started long before we even came to Christ. Before our conversion, we were kept under a cruel tyranny of sin. The Bible tells us that sin has had a "reign in your mortal body" (Romans 6:12), and we were "sold as a slave to sin" (Romans 7:14). We were, "by nature, deserving of wrath" (Ephesians 2:3). It was a cruel and harsh tyranny; a reign of sin that led us away from God and even made us His enemies (Romans 5:10).

With our conversion to Christ, however, we received the

forgiveness of sin, but we still have the influence of sin in our lives. My horrible temper did not go away the day I received Jesus into my life. In some respects, it became worse. Through the years after I was saved, I found a very interesting pattern developing in me. In following my natural inclination, I drifted back into an old habit: I would feel so guilty after sinning that I would attempt to please God by modifying my behavior to be good so that I could compensate for the sin. I attempted more and more to keep the law and found myself judging others who didn't keep it as well as I thought I had. I took up comparing myself with others and, as a result, became either more concerned with pleasing other people by conforming myself to their list or a legalist by pressing others into my mold of what I defined as holiness. Both extremes led me into bondage. Whether a person is a man pleaser or a legalist, he or she becomes bound to keep the whole law and see to it that others do the same.

If we are honest with ourselves, we understand that this is no way to live. We become like schizophrenic Christians who lead double lives; one seen by other Christians at church and the other by those we don't care to deceive. Or, we become miserable people, wondering where we went wrong after starting out so well. Not only does it steal our joy, but it also leaves us feeling we have no real power to influence anyone else by our faith because we feel as though we are complete failures ourselves.

This was the world in which I lived through many years of my life. From the time I came to Christ at age 12, all the way through college, I could not find the answer of how to truly live out my Christian faith. I learned a lot and grew in my relationship with the Lord and with other Christians, but it is only in looking back at this struggle that I can see what I was missing. What I had to understand, what was missing in my life, was a clearer understanding of grace.

After college I attended Dallas Theological Seminary in

Dallas, Texas. Heather and I wanted to go into foreign missions work and I needed more Bible teaching to be better prepared to share God's truths. The first semester I enrolled in a class simply called *Spiritual Life*, taught by Professor William D. Lawrence. It was a required class that many students put off until their last semester. Since it was required, I decided to take it early. An added bonus was that the class wouldn't run the entire semester which would give me more time at the end of the semester to really focus on the classes I assumed would be harder. Little did I know at the time the impact this seemingly easy class would have on my life and the lives of other students.

About halfway through this course, we were discussing the realities of grace and it was clear that nearly everyone in the room was leaning forward in their chairs drinking in these truths. One of my fellow students raised his hand and asked the professor the question we were all thinking, "Why aren't these things taught in the church? Why is this the first time many of us have heard these things?" I don't remember the answer, but I'll never forget the question because I realized that I wasn't the only person experiencing these truths in a profoundly new way.

Some of the lessons in this book are the principles I learned in that class at Dallas Seminary, which, to me, was revolutionary in my life. But those lessons in the classroom were only the beginning. Our very loving and patient God has continued to teach me these lessons over the years since then. That is, after all, where the best and most enduring lessons are learned. I have found that it isn't in the classroom where we learn to understand and appreciate grace, but in our day-to-day walk with God. The classroom or, for that matter, a book about grace, have their place in introducing the concepts we need to understand, but the reality of these truths come out of a living, breathing relationship with Jesus.

As we begin this voyage, I want to ask you to consider a

couple of things. First of all, God has to prepare you to hear it. Please approach these chapters with a lot of prayer. Chances are you have heard many, if not all these things before, but please ask God to show you new depths of understanding. This is a spiritual endeavor, so we have to approach it by seeking His spiritual guidance.

Secondly, you really need to want to know it. It is simply too easy to take our relationship with God for granted. The busyness of life and all the demands we face can lead us away from the most important relationship we have as Christians: our relationship with God. Grace has a way of freeing us in our faith to experience something much deeper. My plea with you is that you will not settle for anything less than an all-out relationship with God, the kind of relationship that is formed when you are completely enthralled with Jesus as you experience the full measure of the grace he has given to you. In order to help you reach that goal, we will dig deeper. The things we'll talk about are fundamental and yet very profound.

The reason for this book is to present how to reach a deeper, more meaningful relationship with God. My heart for any who would read it is to walk away understanding how we, as Christians, can find a deeper intimacy with Him because that is exactly what He wants for us and has designed a way to reach it. It will be different, even opposite, of how we would naturally think to grow in our relationship with Him, at least it was for me. It is based on knowing who we are in the eyes of God, believing and being obedient to what He has said and learning how to remain in Jesus rather than working to please Him out of a sense of obligation or guilt. The book is divided into three sections: Foundations of Grace (basics of grace in the lives of Christians), Delicacies of Grace (recipe for experiencing grace) and Incarnating Grace (practical ways of living in the reality of grace).

Ultimately, I feel as though I had no choice but to write this book. I have personally experienced some of the fullness of God's grace in my life and have attempted to express it in these pages in a most personal way. I wanted to be as transparent and honest as possible so that you, my reader, may see the wonder of grace in my life. My transparency is necessary to give an account of this most precious gem of Jesus' great grace in the life of one man. I believe in order to really understand grace in practical terms is to see it in a life that was in desperate need of it; my life certainly qualifies as precisely that. Perhaps it will encourage you to see this amazing and awesome gem of grace in even the most difficult and shameful parts of your life, too. Jesus came for the sick and broken (Mark 2:17). If you find yourself in that place, this book was written especially for you.

The key to the book is summarized by the title, *Incarnating Grace*. It has to do with the process of allowing Jesus' grace to be released by the Holy Spirit into our lives, and through us, into the lives of others. We are to so radiate His grace that others would see Him living His life of grace through us. Imagine the impact if we, as followers of Jesus, would incarnate His grace in this world that is itself the very incarnation of so much hatred and anger. There is nothing needed more today than grace incarnate.

This teaching, along with a willingness to believe and obey God's word, changed my life completely and forever. If you are ready and willing, it will change your life, too. It is a journey you will never forget nor regret. Who is with me?

Section One – Foundations of Grace (chapters 1-3)

In order to have an appreciation for grace, there are certain things we need to understand about ourselves. This includes not only the good but also the bad. Grace is experienced in the context of both. To truly understand ourselves, we need to grasp fundamental truths to see who we really are at the very core of our being.

CHAPTER 1 - THE NEW HAS COME

2 Corinthians 5:17
"Therefore, if anyone is in Christ, the new creation has come; the old is gone, the new is here!"

As you read through the gospels, you will never once find that Jesus ever uttered the word "grace." Yet, He was the very embodiment of all that grace represents, so much so that the Apostle John describes Jesus as being "full of grace" (John 1:14). Grace is as unfathomable and multi-faceted as the God who gives it. To presume that we understand grace completely would be the furthest stretch of truth imaginable. Yet, a look at the life of Jesus has given me a glimpse of what grace is all about and it makes me realize just how much I need it.

In a nutshell, the most common definition of grace is this: God lavishly giving to us what we don't deserve or could ever earn. That definition is just the tip of the iceberg. Grace runs deep. Its origin is found at the cross of Jesus and reaches anywhere and everywhere that people dwell. It is meant for all, but relatively few ever truly experience it. The self-righteous don't see a need for it and those most needy don't feel worthy enough to receive it. It is always available to us; however, it can only be received with humility and brokenness. Its supply is as vast as an ocean but is measured out according to the need. It is more glorious and breathtaking than even the most majestic mountains.

Think of grace this way: God, the Creator and King of all creation, has determined and is completely committed to give to us all the love and favor (grace) He has to offer. He does not give it based upon anything we can do to receive it or because we deserve it in some way, but simply because He wants to give it. It is part of His character – in His very DNA. Interestingly, of all His creation, we are the only creatures who get to experience grace and yet we may choose to accept or reject it. Even if we do reject it, He is no less willing or less committed to giving it to us.

Perhaps the best way to begin to understand and appreciate grace is to see how it transformed two unlikely candidates: one, a holy, ultra-religious fanatic committed to the tradition of his fathers and the other an ungrateful, entitled son committed only to himself and to his sin. One believed he didn't need grace and the other didn't think he deserved it. All of us fit somewhere within the spectrum between these two characters. Regardless of where we fit in that spectrum, we will discuss the wonder of an amazing facet of grace: new beginnings.

A Man of Extremes

Our first example is a man who was completely committed to destroying any person whom he determined was a follower of Jesus. Saul of Tarsus was confident he was doing the will of God by persecuting Christians and trying to stop the message of the gospel from spreading. He was a hero to the Jews, religious to the core, and ready to stomp out any threat to the faith of his fathers. Few could stand as bold and proud as Saul. And there are few who experienced such a dramatic change in life as he went from Saul, the persecutor, to Paul, the preacher of the very message he tried to destroy.

Saul of Tarsus, "breathing out murderous threats," took his persecution of the church on the road (Acts 9:1-6). He had already thrown many disciples of Jesus into prison in Jerusalem. His hatred toward this new faith was growing as rapidly as Christianity was spreading. But while he was heading to Damascus on a mission of death, he was stopped in his tracks by the Lord of Life. He came face to face with Jesus who essentially told him that to persecute His people was a persecution against He, Himself. This encounter immediately and forever changed the course of Saul's life. He became a missionary just as zealous about spreading the gospel as he had been about preventing the gospel from spreading. We are not told how many believers Saul had put into prison or to death before he became the Apostle Paul, but imagine how he must have wrestled with guilt afterward for what he had done. How could such a person overcome the feelings of shame and guilt that he surely faced?

Paul's answer to this is rooted in his understanding of grace. He states in 1 Corinthians 15:9-10,

> "For I am the least of the apostles and do not even deserve to be called an apostle, because I persecuted the church of God. But, by the *grace* of God, I am what I am, and his *grace* to me was not without effect. No, I worked harder than all of them—yet not I, but the *grace* of God that was with me."

Paul starts off by admitting his guilt for persecuting believers. Humanly speaking, it would have been natural for him to stay in that place and allow it to paralyze him in a cocoon of guilt. But he didn't stay there. Paul so believed in God's grace of forgiveness and new beginnings that he could accept who he was by saying, "I am what I am," without allowing guilt or the enemy to paralyze him. Paul was completely convinced that he was forgiven. He understood that God's grace was infinitely greater than any sin he could ever commit (Romans 5:17). He knew, by faith, that the grace of God given to him had set him free. He was free from the guilt and shame of persecuting the church. The church, in turn, glorified God that Paul, the very one who had persecuted them, was now preaching the gospel he once tried to destroy (Galatians 1:22-24).

Paul became a new creature in a moment of time; the old

passed away and he became someone new. Not only was Paul not the same--the world has never been the same since he became a believer in Jesus. The grace God extended to Paul is the same grace He extends to you and me.

So many have had their own "Damascus road" experience, their pride leading them to think there was no need nor room for God's grace in their lives. Somehow, that grace breaks through to confront the pride and guilt and to bring us face to face with a Savior who is willing to forgive us. Psalm 103:12 tells us, "as far as the east is from the west, so far has he removed our transgressions from us." If He has cast our sin so far away, who are we to bring it up again? He has created in you a new creation; the old things have passed away and new things have come. Think of it this way; the Lord Jesus did not *partially* redeem you when He died on the cross, He redeemed you *completely*. The price was paid in full. Grace and guilt cannot dwell together.

For a few years early in my Christian life, I was plagued by a gripping guilt for a sin that I had committed. There was good reason for this guilt. This one event marked my life forever and has become a defining moment in my understanding of God's great grace because of the severity of this sin. As a young man, I was involved in a relationship with a girl that led to an unwanted pregnancy and later to an abortion that I fully consented to. We broke up not long after and she moved to a different part of the country so we lost touch with one another. It is the darkest part of my life for which I suffered the greatest amount of guilt and shame imaginable. Even though it was behind me and I had confessed it several times, the guilt from that sin kept coming back. It was keeping me from fully living in my relationship with the Lord because I felt that it stood between us.

I finally sought the help of a mentor who asked me if I had confessed this sin to the Lord and I assured him that I had, several times. Then he asked me if I had left it with Jesus and went on to explain from the Scriptures that I was completely forgiven; that I was completely cleansed. That was the beginning of grasping this whole idea of new beginnings. I finally understood that my awful sin, as horrid as it was, was fully paid for at Calvary. I could "do" nothing to be any more forgiven, it was a matter of believing that I "am" forgiven.

God determines the parameters of His forgiveness which began at a very real and tangible blood-stained wooden cross and extends far out beyond any sin we could ever commit, even those as dark and desperate as what I experienced. I still, today, fully embrace His forgiveness knowing that His ever-expanding circles of grace radiating from the cross have reached me right where I am. I have chosen to believe in His forgiveness and not the ever-changing current of my troubled emotions. I rest in the fact that I am a new creation in Christ Jesus. And one day, I will see and hold the child that, quite frankly, I should have been a father to.

I finally found what I needed to restore me back into the most cherished relationship I possess. God, through His grace, gives to us what is needed to handle the guilt and shame that sin brings into our lives. A new beginning means that I can move forward in my relationship with Him, free of shame and guilt. Even though the consequences of our sin may continue, a new beginning means we can rest in His forgiveness and restoration and move forward into a fuller and deeper relationship with Him.

Please understand that the most important part of a new beginning is our willingness to receive His forgiveness. From personal experience, I have found this to be the hardest part of my restoration to Him. I felt as though I didn't deserve to be forgiven. The reason was simple; I would not be willing to forgive me if I were in His place. That, however, is the point - we are not in His place. As we just discussed, we don't determine the parameters of His forgiveness, He does. Until we receive His forgiveness, we will not be free from shame and guilt. His forgiveness is a gift, wrapped in grace, that you can reach out and accept. Don't allow your feelings of unworthiness to hinder you from receiving this gift and the healing that you so desperately need.

It is never too late for a new beginning. Perhaps you have been a Christian for many years yet are still entangled by guilt from a past sin or a sin that has you in its grip right now. A new day can dawn for you by understanding and believing the truth that you are a new creation. He is a God who forgives. Once you have confessed that sin to Him (1 John 1:9) and are willing to be free from its grasp (which we will talk about in the next few chapters) a fresh, new start is waiting for you.

As if it weren't enough, grace goes even beyond our forgiveness. Take a look at the effect that God's grace had upon Paul. In 1 Corinthians 15:10, Paul says that it pushed him to work harder than any of the other apostles. That is what the grace of God, correctly understood, does for the believer. It frees us to live our lives for God. It pushes us to more and deeper service to Him. God's grace motivates us because we understand that we are receiving what we don't deserve, not only forgiveness, but a relationship with God and purpose for our lives. As we will discuss in more depth later in the book, there is no greater motivator than the love that God expresses to us through His grace given by His Son.

Grace for the Wondering

I love the parables of Jesus. Within them He gave us a wealth of truth which so clearly reveals the very heart of God. They show us where His priorities lie, what He values most and gives us a glimpse into His very character. The parable of the prodigal son reveals a lot about God's heart for grace. Anyone who understands grace can identify with the prodigal son's feelings of unworthiness. But there is a thread of hope that is woven through the entire fabric of this story found in Luke 15:11-32 (please read this passage).

Hope is hard to imagine at the beginning of the parable. Normally, an inheritance isn't granted until after the death of the benefactor, but this son asks for his inheritance while his father is living. In essence, this son is saying, "Dad, you're worth more to me dead." Think of the heartbreak of a father who discovers his son values his death more than his life.

The father's heartbreak is worsened as his son leaves with his portion of the inheritance for his own adventures, all of which are far from honorable. This son is bent on living his life as he pleases and to experience sin in the open. Word reaches the family of his loose living with prostitutes which his brother mentions later in the parable (verse 30). Nevertheless, the father sits looking out at the horizon every day hoping for the impossible; that his son will return.

Returning home is the last thing on this son's mind. His only concern is what he can do next to indulge his appetites. He indulges every one of those appetites until his money runs out and reality begins to settle in. His grumbling stomach is a constant reminder to him that his entire inheritance is gone. He then resorts to a job no Jewish boy raised on a kosher diet would ever aspire to: a pig farmer. (You have to love Jesus' sense of humor). While sitting with the pigs, he becomes homesick and starts to think how good life used to be.

At home, he could eat anytime he pleased. His father was a good provider, even for the household servants-- which gave him an idea. Jesus said that, "he came to his senses." He realized that he could not return home as a son, but maybe his father would take him in as a servant.

He gets up, steps out of the pig stye, and begins to make his way home. He smells like a sow and his clothes are torn and tattered. But even worse, he knows he has shamed his father and ruined his own reputation because of his wild living. Nonetheless, he heads home rehearsing the words he will say to his father, "I have sinned against heaven and against you..."

The highlight of the story is when his father catches sight of what he has been longing to see. On the horizon, a sole figure appears that he at once recognizes as his son. His father's heart fills with compassion and he runs to greet his son. Unlike our society, running in public was forbidden in first century Middle Eastern cultures. A grown man never, never ran. If he were to run, he would have to hitch up his tunic (article of clothing much like a robe) so he would not trip. If he did this, it would show his bare legs, which was humiliating and shameful.[2]

As he approaches his son, the father hears the beginning of his rehearsed speech: "Father, I have sinned against heaven and against you. I am no longer worthy to be called your son." The humiliated father stops the speech with the command to the servants to place the best robe, a ring, and sandals on his son. This father shamed himself by racing to cover his son's shame before anyone else could see him. Not only did he cover him, but he did so with his best robe so that no judgment could be made against him. Everyone would recognize that robe as belonging to the father that now covers his son's shame. By putting a ring on his hand, he was identifying him as his own and places a portion of his own dignity on his son which the boy had lost in complete disgrace. The sandals would offer him protection from the world's dirt. Even though he was filthy, smelling like a pig, he was once again welcomed back into his father's home who assumed the responsibility of protecting and restoring him.

With great joy, the father declares a feast and proclaims, "...this son of mine was dead and is alive again; he was lost and is found." It was a new beginning for this boy; death to life, lost to being found. He really was unworthy to receive grace from his father. No one else could understand why he would grant this rebel such grace, not even his own brother as we see later in the story (verses 25-32). But grace is the giving of what we don't deserve. Having received such grace, there was only one thing left for them to do: "So they began to celebrate" (verse 24).

These are two examples of lives turned upside down by grace. One thought he was already on the right path and didn't see the need for grace. The other was convinced that there wasn't enough grace in the world to restore him to his father. Both desperately needed grace. We all find ourselves somewhere on the spectrum between these two people. Whether we recognize it or not, grace is God's solution to the baggage we tend to carry with us. He takes the shame and guilt and covers us with the new self; a robe of dignity, righteousness and restoration (Ephesians 4:24).

A new beginning for us means that God, who knows all things, does not just see us for who we are, but who we will become. I love that. God, in patience and love, looks past the failure to see the potential (1 Timothy 1:12-16). I am so glad that He doesn't look back at the failures of my life and shake His head in disgust, but rather patiently and actively works in my life to conform me into the image of His Son. I'm also glad that He doesn't grant us grace based on our performance but rather on the basis of His person. Grace is simply who He is.

So many of us are hindered, as I have been, by a life that isn't what we have hoped for or are ashamed by the choices we have made in the past. Because of His amazing grace, God is willing to accept each of us just the way we are if we are willing to admit our need for forgiveness and, by His grace, to turn away from the sin that separates us from Him; the very sin for which Jesus died. None of us deserve it, but that is what grace is all about. Grace seeks those who wish to receive it, not based on their good works, who they are or where they are from. It seeks those among us who are sick and need a physician, or those who understand that they are unworthy and stand all by themselves in the back of the church because of their shame. The Father is, right now, looking toward the horizon, waiting for your form to appear and He will run to meet you right where you are. His Son has taken your humiliation and shame on Himself as He hung on the cross. Now, He waits to clothe you with His holiness, to give you a new identity as a new creation, to restore you and to offer to you His protection for all eternity.

Chapter one discussion questions.

1. Discuss your definition of grace as you understand it. What, in your opinion, is the most misunderstood aspect of grace?

2. What did Paul do to combat feelings of guilt he could have had for persecuting the church? How did it free him to serve God the way he did for the rest of his life?

3. Why is a willingness to receive His forgiveness often so difficult? What do you think would be the consequences of not accepting His forgiveness?

4. How has the grace of God impacted your life? What does the fact that you are an entirely new creature in God's eyes mean to you personally?

CHAPTER 2 – OUR IDENTITY IN CHRIST

Ephesians 1:3
"Praise be to the God and Father of our Lord Jesus Christ, who has blessed us in the heavenly realms with every spiritual blessing in Christ."

When you look into the mirror of your life—not the mirror you look into every morning, but the mirror that reflects your own self-image—what do you see? Do you see someone who is perfectly put together but inwardly full of insecurity and fear? Or do you see someone paralyzed by damaging words someone else spoke to you or former failures you experienced? Perhaps you see someone who needs no one else but wishes only to be left alone because of the pain others have inflicted on you. Then there are those who are protective of their own polished image, very obsessive and unwilling to allow that image to alter in the least.

Our identity crisis, whether based on true or imagined ideas about ourselves, has an affect upon us that is real enough. Nothing makes the enemy happier than to point out that distorted image because he knows that if our focus remains toward the mirror, we will never see who we truly are as believers in Christ.

God-Given Identity

Unknown to us at the time, many things transpire the moment we receive Christ as our Savior. The Bible tells us that the angels rejoice (Luke 15:10), our spirits are made alive (Colossians 2:13), our names are written in heaven (Luke 10:20) and we are spiritually removed from the darkness of this world and transferred to the most secure space imaginable (Colossians 1:13). These, however, are not the only benefits we received, we are also given a new identity now that we have been placed "in Christ."

This new identity is something that is given to us by God and it is through this gift that our relationship is opened to Him. Understanding our identity is the key that leads us to understanding God's perception of who we really are. Along with that true perception comes a freedom to serve Him in the things He created for us to do. In other words, once you see yourself for who you actually are, you are free from who you always thought yourself to be and can live in the reality of who God has made you to be.

The Secret to Our Acceptance

The secret that holds the key to understanding God's grace in accepting us is a phrase used many times in the book of Ephesians and in much of the New Testament. That phrase is "in Christ," or often simply stated, "in Him." Such a short prepositional phrase has some huge ramifications tied to it. When you see this phrase in the Bible, think of it as how God actually sees you. The truth that is wrapped in this one little phrase is life changing.

Here are some examples. We are told in Ephesians chapter one that we are blessed with every spiritual blessing in heavenly places "in Christ" (1:3). We were chosen "in Him" before the creation of the world and are no longer strangers to God but adopted into His family (1:4-5). It is "in Him" that we have received redemption and forgiveness of our sins (1:7). We have obtained an inheritance (1:11) and also have been sealed "in Him" with the Holy Spirit of promise (1:13). In other words, we are totally and completely accepted by God for all eternity, and this is the reason why. When we are "in Jesus", we are seen by the Father just as He sees His own Son. Please take a moment and think about that – you are accepted by God the Father just as He has accepted Jesus. As He looks at you, He sees you "in" His precious Son!

Being "in Jesus" places you in a sphere far above this world. You share in all the same rights and privileges of the Lord Jesus because you are "in Him" which now means that you are a child of the King, adopted into His family. Ephesians 2 tells us that God has even raised us up with Jesus and has seated us with Him in the heavenly realms (2:6). This is the place of highest dignity and authority. This is how God our Father sees us.

This is also where our identity issues come into play. As I look at the circumstances in my life, the reality I see is that nothing has changed from who I was before I accepted Jesus. I'm still in the same body, still use the same mind, and have all the same emotions. I'm living in the same country with the same family and some of the same friends. I still struggle with sin and often feel completely lonely and helpless. How is it that the Bible says I am seated with Jesus in heavenly realms, far above this world, when I have so many struggles in my life? How do I reconcile all that I struggle with in living here with the reality of how God sees me?

Allow me to share with you a personal stress reliever. I have had the privilege of living most of my life in one of the most beautiful states in the country. Our mountains in Colorado soar above the prairie with millions of acres of forest and a huge diversity of wildlife. For me and many Coloradans, the mountains are a favorite place to go. When my family and I find just the right spot with no one else around, the trials of life fade as I'm surrounded by the beauty of nature. This experience is precious to me and more valuable than I can express in words. I feel as though I am in a sacred place, the place I meet with God in the most natural way. I may be able to stay only a couple of days, but the effect on me is much longer. Is that spot any less a reality than the stress I face at my workplace or on a drive that takes me into busy traffic? Even though I am not in my sacred mountains continuously, they are still a part of me no matter where I am. You can take the boy out of the mountains, but you can't take the mountains out of the boy.

That is how we can live in the reality of being in Jesus. *He* is our most sacred place. Unlike my example of the mountains, we are continuously *in Him*. Rather than the image in the mirror, He becomes our focal point. The circumstances of life may overwhelm us with stress and anxiety. Our focus may be fixed on the mirror of all the lies we have believed or about our low self-worth or our attempt to be someone we're not, hoping others will not see us for who we truly are. At that point we have a choice to make; either we will remain in that place of defeat or we may choose to rest in our sacred place - in Christ.

Finding the Sacred Place

To find that place of living in the reality of being in Christ, I begin by spending time with Him. Just as I must travel to the mountains to enjoy that sacred place, so I must be willing to give Jesus His place as a priority in my life. Mary, the sister of Martha and Lazarus, found that place at Jesus' feet, listening to His words (Luke 10:39). That is the best place to start. I sit at His feet everyday by reading the gospels, epistles, Psalms or any other portion of the Bible. I learn His perspective on the circumstances I'm facing and look for His real answers to my identity issues.

Sitting at His feet gives me a heavenly perspective. It is from this perspective that we live out our aspirations, our affections, our thinking, and our ways of dealing with the circumstances in our lives. Colossians 3:1-2 challenges us to lift our eyes to see from His heavenly perspective:

> "Since then, you have been raised with Christ, set your hearts on things above, where Christ is, seated at the right hand of God. Set your minds on things above, not on earthly things."

When we determine to give Him the priority and to see our lives from His perspective, He will enlighten our way. When I'm faced with doubt and anxiety, I remember who I am from His perspective as I remind myself from His word of how He sees me. I need His perspective as someone who is in Christ.

So, how do we start? What is required to experience the reality of being in Christ? It all begins when we take a step of faith in believing that what God has said about us is true. Until I believe that I am who He has said that I am, I will not experience the freedom that can be found in Christ. Faith is a step that we must take before we are given the privilege of experiencing the blessings of being in Christ. Otherwise, we will continue to stare at our own reflection and never truly progress in our relationship with the Father. This is actually a matter of obedience – I can take a step of faith by believing God's value of me, of His perception of who I am, or just keep staring at the mirror of who I see myself to be.

For several years, I suffered from depression. As you will read later in the book, my life did not turn out the way I had hoped. I experienced the death of a dream and began to be filled with doubt and frustration over what my life had become. I was my own worst critic and would often run myself down because I hated who I had become. It wasn't until I took steps of faith, one of which was to believe who God sees me to be in Christ, that I began to see the clouds of depression lift. Once I understood how precious I was to God and that He accepts me the way He does His own Son, my perceived failure of who I saw myself to be was replaced by His value of me. Had I not taken God at His word, I have no doubt that I would still be in that very dark place.

Reversing Roles

The incarnation of the Lord Jesus, when God took on human flesh, was the ultimate display of His willingness to identify with humanity. God stepped into our existence in order to walk in our shoes. Jesus, the God of grace, loves you so much that He was willing to become one of us to identify with you. It was the ultimate role reversal.

Think of how terribly difficult it must have been for someone who knew no sin to dwell among people who sin every day. That was, however, just His first step. His ultimate display of identifying with us was His death on the cross as He took our sin upon Himself. The one and only person who knew no sin became sin for us. He went to extreme measures to identify with us so that He could give to us our new identity in Him (2 Corinthians 5:21).

Grace and Our Identity with Christ

I remember early in my Christian experience working so hard for something that I already had. I wanted so much to win the approval of my Heavenly Father that I thought I had to earn that relationship and somehow earn His love and acceptance. Understanding that I had a relationship with the Father because of who I am in Christ, the perfect Son, literally set me free to enjoy that relationship with the Father. There is nothing to earn.

Just hours before His crucifixion, Jesus prayed for those who would believe the message through the testimony of his disciples', a group that includes you and me. Jesus prayed that future generations of believers would be brought to complete unity because "then the world will know that you sent me and have *loved them even as you have loved me* " (John 17:23, emphasis added). The relationship between the Father and Jesus from eternity past was perfect and constant. There is nothing between them to hinder their relationship. It is absolutely perfect (holy) in every way because there is never any sin to hinder it. They never argue, never have conflict or a harsh word. There is never a selfish ambition among them; they absolutely adore one another and are constantly glorifying each other. That is what makes this prayer of Jesus so amazing. The Father actually loves us as He does His Son,

"...loved them as you have loved me." If this weren't written in the Bible, it would be hard to believe, but it is the truth.

The reason that I say this is so hard to believe is that, unlike Jesus, we do bring sin into our relationship with God. We doubt our Father and so often refuse to follow Him. Our sin is before Him every day yet, He loves us just as He loves Jesus in whom He is so well pleased. All of this has come about because of our identity in Jesus. Our only response is to accept the Father's love without doubt and with a heart full of love and worship!

We can finally begin to enjoy a life of peace by leaving behind the worry and anxiety of feeling like we are a disappointment to God or that we have angered Him so much that He would reject us. Just because a child sins against his father makes him no less a child to that father. The same is true in your relationship with God. He will never, ever reject you as His child.

His Goal for You

Romans 8:29 explains God's goal for the lives of each and every one of His children, a work that God set in motion before the beginning of time:

> "For those God foreknew he also predestined to be conformed to the image of his Son, that he might be the firstborn among many brothers and sisters."

As time goes by and you peer into that mirror of your life, the Father wants you to see less and less of yourself as you become more and more conformed to the image of His Son. That is His ultimate purpose for your life. We should see His character, holiness, meekness, boldness, compassion and grace lived out in our lives. We should see His strength, faith, and absolute love and devotion to His Father and to other people lived out in full color before the world. We should see more and more of the image of

Jesus staring back at us (2 Corinthians 3:18). That is, after all, the ultimate goal of what it is to be "in Christ." When we gaze into the mirror, we become the incarnation of grace. That, my friend, is your new identity!

Chapter two discussion questions.

1. Being as transparent as you can, answer this question: what is the image of yourself in the mirror of your life that hinders and keeps you from living free?

2. Discuss how Jesus' coming to identify with us and His death on the cross has the potential to alter the reflection in the mirror. How can these things change your identity?

3. How does our perspective change when we understand that from God's point of view, we are so bound to Jesus that we are seated with Him in Heaven?

4. What freedom do we find when we discover the grace of God given to us in our new identity "in Christ?" How can you now begin to release that old image of yourself as you take hold of who you really are "in Him?"

CHAPTER 3 – THE TRAITOR WITHIN

Romans 7:18
"For I know that good itself does not dwell in me, that is, in my sinful nature. For I have the desire to do what is good, but I cannot carry it out."

"Why did you commit treason?"

"Treason?"

Aldrich Hazen Ames, a CIA operative during the Cold War, repeats the word out loud as if he is shocked by it.

"The word itself sounds evil, doesn't it?" he says. He prefers spying. "It is easier on the ear, exotic even, much more civilized."

During the nine years that he worked for the KGB as a mole, Ames single-handedly shut down the CIA's eyes and ears in the Soviet Union by telling the Russians in 1985 the names of every "human asset" that the U.S. had assigned to work there. In all, he sold the KGB the names of twenty-five "sources." These twenty-four men and one woman, all Russians, were immediately arrested and ten were sentenced to what the KGB euphemistically referred to as vyshaya mera (the highest measure of punishment).[3] This punishment, the article goes on to say, was to be shot in such a way that the executed could not be identified by their facial features.

Ames couldn't bring himself to admit that he was a traitor even though he was a traitor of the worst kind. To have sold out his country and the lives of so many people places him in a category that few deserve. Ultimately, Ames would pay for his treason by a sentence of life in prison regardless of whether he was able to acknowledge what he had done or not.

Whether we are willing to admit it or not we, as believers in the Lord Jesus, also have a traitor in our midst. Actually, the Bible describes this traitor as a very real part of us. This traitor is as devious as Aldrich Ames, perhaps even more so because it never gives up looking for ways to betray us. It knows us thoroughly because it has been present with us our entire lives. The Bible refers to this traitor as the sinful nature.

The Battle of the Spirit and the Sinful Nature

To better understand this traitor, it is important to make some distinctions related to sin which controls the sin nature. To do so, we have to go back to the very beginning, all the way back to creation. We did not inherit "sins" from Adam, we inherited "sin" (singular) from him (Romans 5:12). According to the Vines Dictionary of Old and New Testament words, sin is "an organized power, acting through the members of the body, though the seat of sin is in the will, the body is the organic instrument."[4] Simply stated, sin is a power of the will conducted through the body. It is like a factory out of which sins (the product of sin) are generated. Before you are saved, "sins" are a part of your everyday life because you are controlled by sin itself.

That is not true of the believer in Christ. In speaking of our identity with Him, Romans 6:7 says this about Christians, "anyone who has died has been set free from sin." This is not referring to physical death, but a spiritual death to sin which we will talk about in the next chapter. Notice, again, this is "sin," singular. The power of sin (the factory producing sins) for someone who has trusted Christ has been broken, it is no longer the master.

So, why do we still sin? We sin because we choose to sin. Galatians 5:16-17 says,

> "So, I say walk by the Spirit, and you will not gratify the desires of the flesh (sinful nature). For the flesh desires what is contrary to the Spirit, and the Spirit what is contrary to the flesh. They are in conflict with each other, so that you are not to do whatever you want."

What these verses are saying is that we have the choice to walk in the Spirit or to walk in our sin nature. Our choice is often to sin which says a lot about us. We sin because deep down inside, in our sin nature, there are certain sins we have little intention of giving up. It may be that we tied our identity to some sin, "I come from a long line of drinkers," or, as was said of my grandmother, "She gets angry because she's Irish." (Her temper was legendary, by the way). It seems that by saying those things there is some justification for it, as if it can't be helped. Not only that, but by saying those things we actually give that sin some degree of power over us. It is as if we have sought terms of peace with sin by allowing it into our lives. Whatever the justification, the truth remains that the sin nature only gratifies itself and it finds great gratification in sin.

To begin to understand this battle, let's look at Romans 7:14-25:

> "We know that the law is spiritual; but I am unspiritual, sold as a slave to sin. I do not understand what I do. For what I want to do I do not do, but what I hate I do. And if I do what I do not want to do, I agree that the law is good. As it is, it is no longer I myself who do it, but it is sin living in me. For I know that good itself does not dwell in me, that is, in my sinful nature. For I have the desire to do what is good, but I cannot carry it out. For I do not do the good I want to do, but the evil I do not want to do—this I keep on doing. Now if I do what I do not want to do, it is no longer I who do it, but it is sin living in me that does it. So I find this law at work: Although I want to do good, evil is right there with me. For in my inner being I delight in God's law; but I see another law at work in me, waging war against the law of my mind and making me a prisoner of the law of sin at work within me. What a wretched man

I am! Who will rescue me from this body that is subject to death? Thanks be to God, who delivers me through Jesus Christ our Lord! So then, I myself in my mind am a slave to God's law, but in my sinful nature a slave to the law of sin."

These verses, more so than any other in the Bible, give us a glimpse of the traitor within each and every believer in Christ. From these verses we see the struggle that rages within us. If you've ever wondered why the Christian life is so hard, you will find a part of the answer here. This "Jekyll and Hyde" struggle may leave you wondering if there is any hope to live a life that even begins to resemble true freedom from sin.

When "Doing Good" Isn't Good Enough

Our sinful nature is that part of us that struggles against submitting to God and is only concerned with seeking our own way. Paul uses the imagery of slavery to make his point. This powerful imagery pictures us as having been "sold as a slave to sin." Sin, for its part, is the worst, most harsh slave-owner imaginable. Sin uses it's whip to inflict deep wounds on us emotionally, mentally and physically. We all bear scars from beatings we've received at sin's hand. Yet, as we see from these verses, our nature, as sin's servant, is often more than happy to accommodate sin's desires. That is what makes it so insidious. It truly is the traitor within.

No one knows this better than Christians who struggle with the abuse of alcohol or drugs, who are held by the snare of pornography, or struggle with lust for the same or opposite sex. Any who struggle with these can testify of the intensity and difficulty of this servitude which often began before they gave their life to Christ. But what of those who can't seem to control their temper? What of those who can't help but gossip about others or have a habit of always stretching the truth?

Sin, no matter how we view it - by degrees or severity, shade or color - is still sin. Regardless of our estimation, it is all the same to God. The Bible tells us that the breaking of one of His laws is the same as failing them all (James 2:10). Granted, some sins are much more destructive and carry worse consequences than others, but they are all detestable to a holy God.

The reason why God hates sin isn't because He wants to take away our fun or put a damper on our lives. The reason is because of the destruction it brings into our lives. First and foremost, it is a destroyer of our relationship with Him, a holy and pure God, and He loves us too much to allow any sin to stand between us.

His word tells us, our conscience testifies to us, and the conviction of the Spirit of God within us let us know when we have stepped over the line into sin's territory. As these verses say, we want to do good! That is a desire placed within us when we believe in Christ. But there is another law, a different law, waging war within us and holding us prisoner. We realize that the good we want to do will never be good enough.

Think of an example in your own life. Has God revealed to you an area of sin which you have willingly given over to Him with prayer, dedication and a sincere heart? Have you then set out with resolve to have victory in this area of your life only to be confronted with the temptation again? You tell yourself that you know it is wrong and you are not going to engage in it. However, your mind continues to dwell on it and you suddenly find yourself back at square one, not in victory, but in defeat. You go to God and are truly sorry that you failed once more. You feel remorse for what you have done and diligently confess it in prayer and promise God that you will try harder the next time! But the next time you find yourself even less able to stand and, again, come back to God in defeat. It becomes a vicious cycle of victory then failure followed by shame and guilt. As hard as you may have tried, your efforts to overcome sin have been sabotaged by the traitor, your sin nature. By trying harder, you're actually relying on your own efforts instead of God's grace to overcome the sin you struggle with. The traitor wants you to try harder because along with the trying comes the satisfaction that you can control your sin instead of recognizing that, in reality, it is controlling you.

You wonder how this struggle could happen again and again. To understand it, we need to understand where the war is being fought. Let's look at verse 23: "but I see another law at work in me, waging war against the law of my mind and making me a prisoner of the law of sin at work within me." Quite simply, this is a battle for your mind. The enemy knows that if he can capture the mind, he has what is needed to control the body!

The Choice is Ours

The law of our mind has to do with the choices we make. Because God created us with a will of our own and, as believers, we have the presence of God's Spirit within us, we know what it is to choose between right and wrong. We can intentionally choose to walk away from that sin or we can choose to allow sin to rule our lives. The important thing to notice is that there is a choice to be made. We don't *fall* into sin unintentionally, we *choose* whether or not to do it. If you choose to sin, you will fall again and again and find no freedom in your struggle. Even worse, the consequences of sin always lead to loss. One of the most well-known verses in the Bible appears just previous to these verses and speaks of that loss, "For the wages of sin is death" (Romans 6:23). It may be the death of a relationship or marriage, the death of your witness for Christ, or it may ultimately lead to your physical death. Regardless, the outcome of sin is always loss.

The more I experience failure, the more I understand what Paul is talking about in Romans 7:24, "What a wretched man I am! Who will rescue me from this body that is subject to death?" This is the heart of the battle that rages within us! In my weakness, (in my sinful nature), I surrender to sin and lose all hope that I can ever live righteously before God, to "do good" as Paul states in these verses. Instead, I find myself doing the very things that I hate to do and wonder how I will ever be delivered from it.

But there is hope! Look again at verse 25: "Thanks be to God, who delivers me through Jesus Christ our Lord!" The answer to our struggle is one that can only be solved by God, through our Lord Jesus Christ. Again, notice that Paul does not tell us that if we try harder or make more of an effort we will be delivered from our sinful nature. This is so important for us to understand because that is exactly what we would naturally want to do! We want to solve our own problems, to stand on our own two feet. But, as we shall see, we were never meant to carry that burden. Once we have made the intentional decision to turn away from our sin, we then need help in order to accomplish it.

Resurrection Power

That help, of course, comes from God who never intended for us to accomplish holiness or godliness apart from Him. We were meant to rest upon His power to gain true holiness. Peter speaks about this in 2 Peter 1:3, "His divine power has given us everything we need for a godly life through our knowledge of him who called us by his own glory and goodness." It is by divine power, not your own measly strength, that you can be freed from sin. Because it is divine power, there is no limit to its ability to deliver you. His power comes "through our knowledge" of Jesus, knowledge which comes through a living relationship with Him, and makes it possible to live a godly life. We will talk much more about our relationship with God as a key component for living a godly life later in the book.

Now, however, let's consider the extent of His power. It is infinite and therefore always available to all those who trust in

Him for it. Paul prays that the Ephesian Christians would know God's "incomparably" great power for us who believe. That power is the same as the mighty strength he exerted when he "raised Christ from the dead and seated him at his right hand in the heavenly realms" (Ephesians 1:18-20).

Jesus' resurrection demonstrates the extent of God's power. We think so little of death until we are faced with the finality of death in a personal way. As you gaze upon a lifeless body or touch a lifeless hand, you understand it is nothing more than a cold, empty shell. Jesus had absolutely no life in His body for three days. As with any other death, his body was cold and empty of life. His blood had been completely spilt, His body broken. Then, by the power of God, He was raised from the dead once and forever. God breathed life back into Jesus' body which would never cease to live again. He whose body was dead, completely lifeless, cold and empty rose again to meet His friends, talk to them and even fix them breakfast on the beach (John 21:9-14).

That same enormous power is available to those who are caught in that brutal cycle of failure and shame in their struggle with sin. That is the power we can know and live by today. It may seem like you will never be free from the chains of sin, but the power to overcome is yours if you will take hold of it by faith! Allow this awesome power that raised Jesus to life to enter your life. Just as Paul intended as he wrote to the Ephesians, make it a prayer for your life to know this power that can free you from the sin that holds you. All the demons of hell can't match the power that is "for us who believe." You can claim this power today. Exchange your effort to overcome your sin with the mighty power of God that raised Jesus from death to life. Remember, the power of the resurrection abides in you because He who is the resurrection and the life abides in you (John 11:25).

However, resurrection power only works on a corpse. As long as we are still struggling in our own effort to overcome sin, we are still clinging to our own desire to live our own lives. It is only when we are willing to die to our efforts that the power of the resurrection is available. Only when you are willing to die to yourself, to allow Jesus' life to reign in yours, will the power of the Spirit be available to you. Again, we'll talk more about this later.

Clearing the Title

I don't know of a Christian who isn't tired of the struggle. In its weakness, my nature desires to surrender to sin, allowing it to have dominion in my life. Paul's proclamation of praise that the victory is found "through Jesus Christ our Lord" places a spotlight on what we need to know, first of all, in our struggle for victory over sin. Just as sin has had the dominance, now someone else is needed to take that role. As we said before, we, on our own, were never meant to engage in that struggle. But we first need to understand an essential principle: Jesus is looking for a clear title to your life.

I once owned a Ford Ranger pickup truck. Before selling it, I put over 230, 000 miles on it. I was so comfortable in that truck - the seat conformed to my shape and I knew every sound and smell. I knew how it would handle corners and how much space was needed to safely stop. The day finally came, however, when I knew I had to sell that truck. Even though I was completely comfortable in that little Ranger, I had to give a clear title to the new owner. It was no longer my truck, but his to do with it whatever he wanted - the truck belonged to him.

As strange as it may sound, we can get comfortable with our sin. We know it completely, even though we hate having it in our lives. We conform to it and will even justify it by saying things like, "No one is perfect," or "It's really not that big of a deal." Somewhere along the way, however, we must get serious with our sin and turn over the title of our lives to Jesus. Just like my old pickup, we need to surrender our lives over to Him to do with us as He desires. Just as we were once obedient to sin, now we have the privilege to be obedient to Jesus. He is our rightful owner and master, not the sin we have struggled with our entire lives.

Whose Servant are You?

The Bible is clear that we will serve one of two masters; either we will serve the Lord Jesus or we will serve sin, it is as simple as that (Romans 6:16). The idea of being a servant or a slave is so contrary to our thinking in this society today. On a radio call-in show, I once heard a man saying he didn't like the whole idea of being a servant of God, but loved seeing himself as a child of God. We enjoy the idea of seeing ourselves as God's children and there is nothing wrong with that because that is who we are. But the fact remains that we are also servants, having been bought with a price with nothing less than the blood of Jesus. We are not as independent as we would like to believe—we are to be slaves to righteousness. It is no mistake that Paul declares our victory "through Jesus Christ our LORD" (emphasis added).

Because we are under the dominion of either the power of sin or the power of Jesus, it is essential that we begin to see ourselves as we truly are, servants of our Master, servants of Christ. This can be best understood by looking at an example in the Old Testament of what it was to be a servant (some translations use the word bond-servant) of a very good and loving Master.

God details the slave-master relationship in Deuteronomy 15:12-17:

> "If any of your people—Hebrew men or women—sell themselves to you and serve you six years, in the seventh year you must let them go free. And when you release them, do not send them away empty-handed. Supply them

liberally from your flock, your threshing floor and your winepress. Give to them as the LORD your God has blessed you. Remember that you were slaves in Egypt and the LORD your God redeemed you. That is why I give you this command today. But if your servant says to you, "I do not want to leave you," because he loves you and your family and is well off with you, then take an awl and push it through his earlobe into the door, and he will become your servant for life. Do the same for your female servant."

God established the opportunity for a Hebrew experiencing a financial hardship to approach his wealthy neighbor and to offer his services to labor as a servant. This passage lays out the parameters of his service, which include an opportunity for the slave to have his freedom restored after six years. When the slave departed, the wealthy master was to provide blessings for the slave, reflecting appreciation for the years he or she worked for the master. It seems the master was instructed to celebrate the years of faithful service before sending the servant on his way.

But this passage also makes provision for the servant who wanted to stay. It could be that the servant would choose to stay with his master. Perhaps it was because he realized his value to his master's household, or because he had everything he needed and was fully taken care of which wouldn't be the case if he left. Motivated by love toward the master, this servant had the option to offer himself for a lifetime of service.

In this case, a very different ceremony would occur. I imagine the entire household gathering at the entry door where the servant would explain his or her intention to remain in service to this kind master and his house for the rest of their days. Then the servant would place his head next to the door post where his ear would be pierced with an awl signifying the permanence of this service. From then on, he would be recognized as the "servant" of this kind master for the rest of their life.

The beauty of this story is found in the person who makes a surprising choice. Who is it that initiates this bond? It is the servant who volunteers himself for a lifetime of service. His love and admiration for his master led him to choose service to this man over his freedom. His decision to stay speaks volumes of his feelings toward his master. He found in him something more precious than even his freedom. He found in his master someone to love and trust.

The Greek term in the New Testament for this kind of servant is translated "Doulos" which means, "one devoted to another to the disregard of one's own interests."[5] No longer does this slave live for himself, he commits the remainder of his days to his master and disregards himself and his own interests for the sake of the one he serves.

Our sin nature entices us to follow the wrong master today. Sin has an arsenal of weapons to use against us. Only you know the "would be" enticements that call after you. Jesus is the only One who can save us not only from our sin but also from ourselves — from our sinful nature.

In the book of Romans, Paul introduces himself as "Paul, a servant (doulos) of Christ Jesus..." Not only Paul but also Timothy, Peter, John and even James and Jude, half-brothers of Jesus, used this word to declare themselves servants of Christ. They found in Him a kind Master, one who met their every need. He accepted them with all their imperfections and gave them a purpose and hope. True to that purpose as His servants, they devoted themselves to their Master, the Lord Jesus, to the complete disregard of their own interests.

The point of all this is that once Jesus receives the rightful place in the center of our love, the love we have for the things that our sinful nature desires begin to diminish. Our affection for what we once craved through that nature is replaced with a heartfelt desire to please our new Master, the one we love. Old desires are replaced with new ones.

I will be the first to testify that this does not happen overnight and it is a daily struggle. However, what I notice in my own life is that those sins I struggle with are not nearly as difficult to turn away from as they once were. I know that the desire of my Master is to maintain a living relationship with me, and He has given me the divine power to turn from those things my sin nature entices me to do. I also know that Jesus keeps his promises, sin never does. Sin will satisfy in the short run but will only bring devastation in the long haul. Jesus will never disappoint us. He gives us exactly what we need when temptation to sin arises.

Forgiven Much, Loved Much

I, of all people, know how much I've been forgiven. Because I have been forgiven much, I love much. His grace becomes to me the most precious commodity I possess; so much more than the sin my nature craves. The love I have for my Savior gives me the motivation to turn from that sin. Placing my faith in Jesus' power enables me to do it.

We understand that there has never been a Master as good and kind as the Lord Jesus. There is nothing that we need that He does not provide. I see it as totally reasonable to devote myself to Him to the complete disregard of my own interests. He has placed the highest priority on us and proved it by dying for us. Imagine, the only true and rightful Master of all things, the Creator of you and me, dying for us, his servants. There is none that can compare to Him. Such love makes giving Him His rightful place on the throne of my heart a very easy decision.

Chapter three discussion questions.

1. How does the imagery of our sinful nature as a slave to sin help to define our struggle with sin in our lives?

2. Think for a moment of a sin that you have struggled to overcome. At what point do you engage your mind when confronted with the choice of whether or not to give in to that sin?

3. What is involved to move us from the point of struggling to overcome our sin ourselves to allowing His "divine power" to deliver us from it?

4. To truly overcome sin, we must give to the Lord Jesus the role of Master in our lives. How is it that giving Him that place enables us to begin to be delivered from sin? Are you at the place in your life that you would consider yourself to be His servant?

Section Two – Delicacies of Grace (chapter 4-6)

God's grace is a wonder to behold – it provides not only for our salvation but also for our daily walk with Jesus. It is the one constant all through our lives that is absolutely necessary to enjoy an intimate relationship with Him. As we all know, there are obstacles which can hinder this walk. This section will deal with Romans 6, a chapter that so clearly draws our attention to the way God designed for us to walk in His grace. In it, we gain understanding of how to overcome the biggest obstacle in our relationship with Him which is our sin.

CHAPTER 4 - INGREDIENTS FOR HOLINESS

Romans 6:6
"For we know that our old self was crucified with him so that the body ruled by sin might be done away with, that we should no longer be slaves to sin..."

If you have ever tasted a cake or pastry missing an important ingredient, you will sympathize with this story. For a season of our lives, Heather and I lived overseas in Eastern Europe. I remember walking down the quaint cobblestone streets of the city where we lived and looking into the windows of tiny cafes to see the most absolutely delicious looking pastries you have ever seen. But, as we found out, looks can be deceiving. I remember so clearly the first time we bought a couple of those wonderful looking morsels. After anticipating a sweet, tasty treat, we were completely disappointed after our very first bite. Though they looked as inviting as any pastry we'd seen in the States, they contained probably half the sugar of an American pastry and were, in our estimation, bland at best. (Our European friends would often eat the cake portion of a chocolate cake and leave the frosting because it was, "so sweet." I never understood that). It wasn't until we tasted the pastry that we discovered that these beautiful desserts weren't tasty at all because they were missing what made pastries we loved so appealing; the sweetness like those we enjoyed at home. They were nothing more than bland pastries that didn't live up to our expectations.

Scripture clearly describes the ingredients for living a full Christian life. Some believers who are in a constant struggle with sin may think this to be an empty hope, much like the pastries Heather and I were so excited to gobble up but became so sorely disappointed in. The hope is that simply becoming a Christian would take care of anything that might get in our way of really enjoying a relationship with God. But, as we said earlier, becoming a Christian may actually intensify our struggle. However, if we were to take as ingredients the teaching in Romans 6 and stir them with faith, they would blend into a wonderful reality of living life as God intended for us. For many of us, our problem is that we allow our experience to dictate what we believe instead of believing God's word and allowing it to dictate our experience.

The Invisible Rope

A TV documentary I saw some time ago featured domesticated elephants of India. It showed a man placing nothing more than a small rope around the leg of an adult elephant which completely immobilized the giant. At any moment, the elephant could have walked away, easily breaking the rope but instead it was kept tethered until the man returned to take it off. It was explained that when the elephant was small, it was tied to a rope that it struggled against until its leg was sore and bleeding. After several days, the elephant accepted defeat and stopped struggling. Since that time, it took only a small rope to keep the largest of all land animals tethered because experience had taught the elephant not to even attempt to break free, even though freedom in the jungle was only a tug and a few steps away.

Sin has wounded us all deeply, so much so that many believe they cannot be free of it. No matter your past, you can be liberated because as we said in the last chapter, *you have died to sin* (Romans 6:2). In Christ we have all that we need to break the invisible rope and be freed from it. I don't mean to minimize your struggle with sin, but if the struggle is your sole focus, you are focusing on the wrong thing.

That is why Paul gives us a couple of simple ingredients in Romans 6 that place our focus in the right place. If our focus is right, we will have what is needed to live a life that is freer, fuller and fulfilling because it leads to a life that enjoys a richer relationship with God. The ingredients are actually facts that we must implement into our lives. In this chapter, we will look at one ingredient about ourselves and one ingredient about Jesus that we must know.

Romans 6:6-7 tells us:

> "For we *know* that our old self was crucified with him so that the body ruled by sin might be done away with, that we should no longer be slaves to sin— because anyone who has died has been set free from sin."

Before any change in life can occur, we need to know a few things. The first concept for us to grasp is knowing, "that our old self was crucified with him." To begin with, we must know our identity with Christ to the point of knowing that we died when He died. Think of yourself as being at the cross when Jesus died. In the eyes of God, that is exactly where you were. Actually, you weren't a spectator that day, you were a participant. When you see yourself in your struggle with sin, you need to see nails driven through your hands and feet. You need to see your old self, the person that was ruled by sin, as crucified on a cross with Jesus. Paul spoke about this to the Galatians, "Those who belong to Christ Jesus have crucified the flesh (sinful nature) with its passions and desires" (Galatians 5:24).

For all who would place their faith in Christ, we must know that the old self that was ruled by sin died with Him on that day. The old is gone. As we see in 2 Corinthians 5:17, the beauty of the new creation is that "if anyone is in Christ, the new creation has come: *The old has gone*, the new is here!" (emphasis added). You are not who you once were but as we said in chapter 2, you are completely new. The old person you once were died with Him but the new person that you are now is raised to life.

The Power of Sin is Broken

As we discussed in chapter 3, we were placed on the slavery block and sold to sin. Now, through His sacrifice, Jesus has purchased us back from sin. Imagine Jesus, looking at us who are so hopeless and helpless, stepping forward to say that He would purchase us lock, stock and barrel. That is exactly what took place that dark day when He died at Calvary.

But here is the part that you don't want to miss! Not only was the body held by sin done away with, so was the *power* of sin over that body, just as we read in Romans 6:7, "because anyone who has died has been set free from sin." We generally don't think of death as liberating unless we consider someone being set free from a disease with which they had suffered. My mom had a stroke a couple of years before she passed away. During that time, she had other health issues that made it very hard for her to get through each day because of the constant pain she was in.

I remember the day she died experiencing that hollow feeling of the loss we had just sustained. There is no one who can replace your mother. Then, I thought of her perception of what she had just stepped through. Not only was she in the presence of her Savior, but she was also free of the pain that had made her life so unbearable. The pain had no more power over her.

Sin is a disease that ravishes the body. It is merciless and ultimately leads to death (Romans 6:23). However, its power is broken by the death of our old self. The finality of death has broken any chance sin might have had to dominate you. Anyone who has died has been set free from the power of sin!

However, before you can experience freedom, you need to first know sin's power over you is broken. You have been liberated, set free, from the power of sin! The reason we can have

such confidence is because of the next thing that we need to *know*; the thing we need to know about Jesus.
Romans 6:8-10 tells us:

> "Now if we died with Christ, we believe that we will also live with him. For we know that since Christ was raised from the dead, he cannot die again; death no longer has mastery over him. The death he died, he died to sin once for all; but the life he lives, he lives to God."

We must also *know* the awesome power of the God we serve. This second ingredient, the one thing we need to know about Jesus, is that He came to free us from sin. "He died to sin once for all," which means the penalty for sin was paid in full, once and forever. And, having done that work, He now lives to God. His life today is a confirmation that the power of sin in our lives was defeated and the proof of that is in His resurrection.

Speaking of His life in John 10:18, Jesus said, "No one takes it from me, but I lay it down of my own accord. I have authority to lay it down and authority to take it up again. This command I received from my Father." Jesus' death and resurrection was in God's plan from the beginning. He used death for His own purposes and plan. His purpose in dying was not only to remove the power of death from us but also the power of sin from us. We, as Christians, often praise God because death no longer has power over us. We know we have eternal life because of His sacrifice on the cross and His resurrection. But seldom do we recognize the fact that sin no longer rules over us.

I fear that we, as believers, don't appreciate this truth nearly enough. I so often attempt to wrestle against sin in my own strength as though it had the upper hand rather than knowing and believing that it has no power over me at all. Just like the elephant tethered to the post by a small rope, we don't realize that the power of sin was defeated by our all-powerful Savior. The awesome power of Jesus has defeated both the power of death and the power of sin over us.

Overwhelming Power

Imagine speaking to a citizen of Poland in 1939 about the German army. I'm sure they would have told you that there was no power that could overcome Germany especially after their country was overrun in just over a month. The power of the German war machine must have overwhelmed them. However, less than a decade later, the German army lay completely in ruins at the hands of the Allied forces. This power that seemed so invincible was defeated by a power even greater than what those Polish citizens witnessed in 1939.

The same is true of Jesus' power to overcome our sin. That great power that has overwhelmed us for so long is totally annihilated by the power of our Savior and, as we said in the last chapter, we now live by the power that was so overwhelmingly displayed in the resurrection.

When we are in the middle of the struggle with some sin, it is so important for us to focus on what we know: that He has defeated sin. If we could just get our eyes off ourselves and place them on Jesus, we would begin to see the victory. But, if I sit in defeat and yield to the "inevitable next failure," I can't expect to see victory because my focus is entirely in the wrong place.

It is essential that we deal with sin the way He has commanded us to in His word. We must repent of sin which means we are to turn completely away from it and head in the opposite direction (Mark 1:14-15). Sin does not match who we are in Christ. We must also recognize that sin destroys our relationship with God and confess it to Him (1 John 1:9). He promises to forgive and cleanse us completely. We are to continue to walk before Him cleansed as those who are vessels of honor by fleeing from lust and pursuing righteousness (2 Timothy 2:21-22).

Generally speaking, most of us have been taught these things, but it doesn't end there. We also must apply our faith by believing that He has enabled us to have victory over sin because of one reason – *He* has had victory over sin! And, because He has, we have, too.

Knowing and Believing, Hand in Hand

It is no coincidence that Paul uses the word, "believe" in this passage. Romans 6:8, "Now if we died with Christ, we *believe* that we shall also live with Him" (emphasis added). It is not enough just to know these facts, we apply what we know by believing that what God has said is true. Knowledge and faith must go hand in hand otherwise our knowledge is meaningless. Faith is only as good as the one in whom you place it. Our faith begins with what we know, and it is based on none other than the Person of God. He knows exactly what we need and is willing to provide it through His grace.

Let's say that you are faced with heart surgery. You naturally will want the best surgeon you can find. You will want to be certain that he has done the procedure you are facing many times before with a stellar success rate. Imagine that you found such a surgeon and met with him for your pre-op meeting to discuss the procedure and you began to inform him of how you would like the operation to go. You tell him the instruments you want him to use and how you envision he should make the incision and what needs to happen once he encounters the blockages he finds. That would be ridiculous, right?

At some point, you must listen to the expert on heart surgery and what he sees is the best way to proceed. You must trust that he knows what he's doing and yield to his wisdom. The same is true in our struggle with sin. Nowhere in the New Testament are we told to fight against sin in our own strength or make more effort to overcome it. At some point, you will need to trust the One who is capable of dealing with what you were never meant to handle. He will do heart surgery on you, but His method is not to eliminate blockages, but to give you a complete heart transplant. Ezekiel 36:26 says,

> "I will give you a new heart and put a new spirit in you; I will remove from you your heart of stone and give you a heart of flesh."

The first ingredient is *knowing that the old self was crucified with Him* and that we have been raised with Him in victory over sin. His resurrection is proof that He has defeated sin. As a believer in Jesus, you, too, have emerged with Him from the tomb. You are a new creature with a new spirit and a new heart. The body of death is taken away, "The old has gone, the new is here" (2 Corinthians 5:17).

The other ingredient is *knowing the power of the One who was sacrificed for us.* We can have confidence in knowing that He has defeated sin because of the power He displayed in the resurrection. Because we are in Christ and because He lives, we have life, not only in the future for eternity, but a full life right now in our walk with Him (John 10:10). I have no power to deliver myself from the power of my sin. If I could, there would have been no need for a Savior and there would have been no reason for Jesus to have died on the cross (Galatians 2:21). What I must do is to believe what I know to be true and to seek God's power working through me to deliver me from sin's power.

I love to watch my wife add all the ingredients needed to bake her chocolate cake (mainly because she will let me lick the bowl after the batter has been poured into the pan.) I know instantly if something is missing. However, when all the right ingredients have been added, she mixes it all together and puts it into the oven to bake. I don't understand how all the ingredients come together to make that wonderful cake, I'm just glad when it's in the oven and can't wait to sample that wonderful taste.

Chapter four discussion questions.

1. What is the hardest part of allowing the Bible to dictate our experience rather than allowing experience to dictate what we believe?

2. How can we know that we have been crucified with Jesus - what is necessary to live in the reality of what God says is true about us and what we see as the reality in which we live everyday?

3. How might you approach your struggle against sin after knowing that you have died to it? Discuss what role your faith in Jesus' awesome power plays in freeing you from the power of sin.

4. What is the difference in fighting against sin in my own strength and allowing God to fight this battle for me? Why do you suppose allowing Him control in this part of life can be so difficult to do?

CHAPTER 5 - STIRRING IN THE INGREDIENTS

Romans 6:11
"In the same way, count yourselves dead to sin but alive to God in Christ Jesus."

If the ingredients for our faith come through our *knowledge* that we have died to the power of sin so that we can live by the power of Jesus' life, then the process of stirring those ingredients together is the next step in claiming grace to overcome sin. Stirring in the ingredients has to do with applying the things we know to be true by looking at what could become our reality. Let me explain. We are given permission to explore the impossible, to dream big as to what our lives could be. In order to fully understand what we've learned about grace (and to begin anticipating a new, victorious life in Christ) we must *count* (or consider) what it means to be "dead to sin but alive to God in Christ Jesus" (Romans 6:11).

Dead to One: Alive to Another
In the Greek, to count means, "to take account of – to figure, count or compute."[6] It is an accounting term. This portion of our sanctification blends with what we need to know. As we saw in the previous chapter, we know that we died with Christ and were raised with Him so that we can live to God. Now, we need to count or calculate what our life will be should we choose to die to sin.

What exactly is it that we are supposed to count, consider, or calculate? This is an essential component with our battle against sin. First of all, we are to count ourselves as dead as a corpse to sin. Just imagine sin poking and prodding a corpse to no response.

That is a great way to view our battle with it. I am a huge fan of the *Lord of the Rings* film series. For whatever reason, when I think of sin prodding a corpse, I see the creature Golem with a stick poking away at a dead body to no response. Sin loses all its power over my body when I consider myself to be dead to it. Dead is dead after all. But, realistically, what does that look like? If sin has dominated your entire life, can you just shut it off?

The key to this verse is to understand our placement. The second fact we must consider from this verse is that we are "alive to God *in Christ Jesus*" (emphasis added). It is in His life that I find the proven power to overcome sin. Again, Jesus' resurrection is the proof of His ability to overcome and it is by that same power that I am placed alive in Christ. I don't have the power within myself to fly to Europe within a day's time, but put me inside a Boeing 787 and I can get there. The Lord Jesus has overcome the enemy of sin for us and, because we are placed in Him, we share in His victory. God, who sees your full potential, wants you to count the implications of living in the reality of that potential!

And, just as we are dead as a post to sin, we are now made even more alive to God. Freedom from the power of sin should generate within us life at its fullest. Once we begin to understand the extent of our liberation, life takes on a whole new meaning. This truth allows us to see beyond our mountain of struggle to the sanctuary where God intends for us to reside as we live to Him.

Dream Big

In the process of considering something, we step from the theoretical "knowing" about an issue, which we talked about in the last chapter, into the practicality of how to live it out. In other words, I go from knowing a truth to considering what that truth means to me personally and how it will impact my life. I need to ask myself, "In what ways, as I consider being dead to sin but alive to God in Christ Jesus, will this truth affect me? Will it have any effect upon my life at all? What will all of this look like?"

Before making changes in my life, I want to think about what those changes will look like down the road. Just like a student leaving home for college or someone starting a new job, we want to think about what this change in life will look like for us. Change is difficult enough, so considering a desired result is an important part of making the adjustment. This is especially true when you consider finding freedom from a sin that has dominated your life. It's a starting point for finding freedom.

This is when you should allow yourself to dream big. What is the impossible life you wish you could live? What is it that you would like to see happen or that you believe your Father would like to see for you? I'm not talking about the possessions you could own or the desire to find happiness or health that can be taken away in a moment of time. I'm talking about your relationship with God and your family or friends. True fulfillment comes with the things that go beyond the temporal to those that are eternal. Proof of that is found sitting in the chair next to a death-bed and hearing the last words of someone about to die. Rarely will they lament not purchasing a Ferrari, but will agonize over a broken relationship.

Perhaps it's the anger you express to your kids when they push you to the limit, or the distractions in life that lead you away from a relationship with God. That distraction could be as simple as filling your days with sport activities or your hours of screen time in social media, TV, or gaming. Both men and women are trapped in the snare of pornography today. It may involve the substance you've come to depend on to get you through the day. It may be the conflict you have with a neighbor or someone at work.

Consider what it would be like if the kids push you to that limit, but they hear no explosion of words. That distraction that eats up so many hours of your day is managed so that you can nurture your relationship with God, family and friends or the drugs or alcohol tucked away in some drawer is thrown out for good. Sexual images that invade your mind are surrendered to the Father who cleanses you whiter than snow. That person you hated is now someone you are able to share a laugh with. The only way these things can become a reality is to consider the benefits of dying to your right to retaliate or to decide to give your time to something that has true, lasting value. Counting the cost of what you will lose can never compare to the riches of being alive in Christ. He is a treasure infinitely more valuable than the distraction or substance that you thought was necessary to get you through the day.

I want to challenge you to consider opportunities this truth can give to you. This has some deep implications for us. From this time forward until the end of your life, count where you can be in your relationship with the Savior if you believed yourself to be dead to sin, but alive to Him and living your life for Him and for His glory. Teenagers, calculate where you can be in your relationship with your parents because you are dead to sin, but alive to God. Couples should consider what your relationship with your spouse could be if you are dead to sin, but alive to God. Parents and grandparents, count for yourselves the heritage you can leave for your children and grandchildren as they see you living as dead to sin, but alive to God. Consider how those things, witnessed by your family and friends, will change them forever.

Calculate how that kind of life could change and impact so many other lives you will have the opportunity to touch because you have lived as dead to sin, but alive to God. This could be your life – a life that is changed and can be used to change so many other lives!

However, this is where you must make the calculation - you must ask yourself if the trade is worth it to you. You can stay in the same place and make no changes at all or you can choose to step forward in God's grace and by His enablement to live a life that is different. Jesus encouraged His disciples to count the cost of following Him (Luke 14:25-33). The Christian life is not meant to be a common life. You can do whatever it is He is asking you to do. The place to start is to rid yourself of that sin that you know is standing between you and your Father by considering that you are dead to sin, but alive to God in Christ Jesus.

A warning is needed here. If you are struggling with a sin in your life it will be necessary for you to consider the result of making no changes and allowing that sin to continue. We have much to lose should we refuse to surrender it to God. If we remain alive to sin we risk becoming as dead to God. He will not use those who willingly and knowingly have chosen the temporary pleasure of sin over a full and fulfilling life spent with Him. Even worse, sin leads in only one direction; it will only lead to death (Romans 6:23). We must understand that our sin affects not only ourselves, but others as well. The destruction it brings has the potential to destroy those we love the most. Don't allow it to take your marriage, family, relationships, health or life because you refuse to make the changes you know you need to make.

Count the Sacrifice - Looking Around

If you are serious about being alive to God in Christ Jesus, then you will also need to take into consideration other things besides sin that may be holding you back. It is sometimes difficult to let go of possessions, habits, and people that you knew before living to God, but it may be the very thing that you need to do.

I made a profession of faith at the age of twelve, but I did not consider what that really meant to me for several years. After high school, I would try to share my faith with some of my friends, but still go to parties on Saturday night before attending church on Sunday. It was a half-life that was really no life at all. This went on until one spring afternoon at the age of 19 when a friend invited me to ride motorcycles to a motocross track. There were so many things that happened that day which point to the fact that the Lord was protecting me and giving me the opportunity to consider His role in my life.

For instance, before the ride, my friend handed me a helmet and told me to put it on. I told him that I never wore helmets, which was true. My oldest brother gave me a dirt bike that I rode during my years in high school and I never bothered to wear a helmet at all during that time. My friend told me that if I didn't wear a helmet, I would not ride with him.

It had been about a year since I had last ridden my bike and my friend was a lot better at handling motorcycles than I was. We took off on some winding back roads on our way to the track which I would never reach. After a series of sharp turns, I got off the road into some gravel which pulled me even further off the road. I ended up hitting the bank of a ditch which propelled me through the air to a very hard landing. When all the dust had settled, I had a ruptured spleen, collapsed lungs and a helmet that was cracked straight down the middle.

My friend saw it all happen and came back to help. He knew that I was in big trouble, so he flew on his bike to a nearby home and called an ambulance. They arrived within 10 minutes of the accident, another way I saw the Lord's hand of protection on me that day. My collapsed lungs gave me only very short, labored breaths.

After surgery, I was in the hospital for about a week. During that time, a group of my party friends came to see me. As much as I liked those guys, it would be the last time I would see many of them. I would have loved for them to have come to Christ, but our lives separated at that point which was as much their choice as it was mine. I knew the Lord had laid claim on my life and that I was to live for Him. On that day, I understood what Paul meant when he wrote something very profound in his letter to the Philippians; my life was changed, and I had to consider all that I was before the accident to be lost. I could not have gone back to the person they knew me to be.

This is some of what Paul had in mind as he wrote in Philippians 3:7-9:

> "But whatever were gains to me I now consider loss for the sake of Christ. What is more, I consider everything a loss because of the surpassing worth of knowing Christ Jesus my Lord, for whose sake I have lost all things. I consider them garbage, that I may gain Christ and be found in him, not having a righteousness of my own that comes from the law, but that which is through faith in Christ—the righteousness that comes from God on the basis of faith."

Just like Paul, I realized that the lifestyle I used to value was worthless, it was actually a loss and not a gain, because of the "surpassing worth of knowing Christ Jesus my Lord." It was at this point in my life that I finally began to lose other things in order to gain Christ.

Reaching the Goal - Looking Ahead

Paul had considered all in his past as loss for Christ's sake. All his credentials and the pride of his own self-righteousness he considered to be garbage compared to knowing his Savior. Whether we are ashamed of our past or prideful in our self-righteousness, notice how we all attain true righteousness. Paul said, "…not having a righteousness of my own that comes from the law, but that which is through faith in Christ—the righteousness that comes from God on the basis of faith" (verse 9). This eliminates any self-effort (as if it's all up to me) that I may put forth to be righteous. Just as I, by faith, reached out to God for salvation, so I must also, by faith, reach out to God for sanctification.

Our consideration of our past, whether good or bad, as an

issue of pride or of shame, must be set behind us. The Lord does not want us to dwell on what we were, but desires that we push forward. Lying in that hospital bed and the days that followed in my recovery gave me a lot of time to think. I realized that my popularity with my friends became a shame to me as I considered the value of my relationship with Jesus. Back to our passage, Romans 6:21 says, "What benefit did you reap at that time from the things you are now ashamed of? Those things result in death!" It is time to put behind us the things that make us ashamed when we place them in light of our relationship with Jesus.

Following Paul's example, we must set our minds on the goal ahead of us, and calculate the distance to reaching that goal. Then we must, like Paul, set off in pursuit of that goal. Listen to how he describes his pursuit in Philippians 3:12-14:

> "Not that I have already obtained all this, or have already arrived at my goal, but I press on to take hold of that for which Christ Jesus took hold of me. Brothers and sisters, I do not consider myself yet to have taken hold of it. But one thing I do: Forgetting what is behind and straining toward what is ahead, I press on toward the goal to win the prize for which God has called me heavenward in Christ Jesus."

Faith is the Fuel, Change is the Engine

It requires faith to count ourselves dead to sin. Faith means taking those things which God has said and claiming them for our own. Faith looks into the future and says, "By God's grace, this is what my life will be." Ask God in faith to show you those things in your life that are not compatible as His follower. Then, once He reveals what must change, press ahead believing He will make it happen. It means being willing to turn away from the past and its failures to the bright hope of what He would like to see in you. Above all, take hold of Him in faith because you can count on Him!

Our consideration also requires change. We won't get from point A to point B by projecting our faith toward a future goal and hoping it will come to pass. For Paul to have advanced, he said he had to calculate the changes he needed to make by releasing certain things from his grasp which enabled him to reach forward toward the prize. He had to let go in order to reach ahead which meant that he had to count the cost. Those changes in our lives may be drastic or quite subtle. If you are taking steps in your walk with Christ, He will reveal the changes that need to take place to reach the goals He has set for you.

There are some relationships that you will not be free to simply release as I did with my party friends. For instance, you will have to trust Him to make needed changes in your relationship with a spouse or family member. However, witnessing the changes you are making as you consider yourself dead to sin but alive to God may challenge them to make changes in their own lives as well. Those changes, along with your prayers, may be the very thing they were needing to witness to understand their need for Jesus (1 Corinthians 7:12-16, 1 Peter 3:1-2).

Not only will our consideration require change, it will also require courage. It can be very scary to consider making changes in our lives. I find myself very comfortable in what I know; in how I live my life on a day-to-day basis even in times when I know it is not where I should be. To consider making changes by letting go of sin, people or things that I know He wants me to release from my life requires a lot of courage. He can give you the courage you need. There is an unlikely place where I have found the courage to die to sin and live to Him. I have found that courage is available through worship. As I worship, I place my eyes on Him alone and, as I step into His presence, fear flees and courage takes its rightful place in the presence of the King.

Consideration that Leads to Worship

In the end, our consideration of what our life might be and what we will need to release will become a wonderful expression of worship to God. This is the topic of the next chapter. Once you seat Him in the place He alone deserves by surrendering the changes you need to make, you are offering to Him the truest form of worship. It is as though you are counting Jesus of more value than any substance, distraction, emotion, person or anything else that gets in the way of your relationship with Him. He will, in exchange for those things, give to you true freedom (John 8:34-36). In worship, we see things as they truly are. Jesus alone is worthy of preeminence in our lives. Anything else that competes with Him is a waste of life. Whatever it may be, count Him to be of much more value and release it to Him. Dream big as you consider yourself now dead to sin, but alive to God in Christ Jesus.

Chapter five discussion questions.

1. What is the difference between hoping you can overcome a struggle with sin and considering yourself to be dead to it?

2. Do you personally know someone who lives as though they understand the concept of being dead to sin but alive to God? If you do, how would you describe their life?

3. What is it that God has shown you that you need to consider yourself to be dead? How will your life change should you choose, by faith, to see yourself as dead to that sin, person or possession and alive to God?

4. Is there something you need to release in order to reach ahead to claim the prize of God's upward call on your life?

CHAPTER 6 – BAKING THE DELICACY

Romans 6:13
"...offer yourselves to God as those who have been brought from death to life..."

After the ingredients have been added and stirred, the delicacy of grace needs to be baked. This is one of the most anticipated moments of the process, just like when Heather bakes her chocolate cake. After the runny ingredients are poured into the pan and then placed into the oven, they combine to transform into a soft, moist cake. The smell of those baked ingredients, mixed together, begin to fill the house and my taste buds ignite as I anticipate the wonderful taste of that delicacy. I find myself so close to the oven door that I can feel the heat at the end of my nose.

Total Allegiance

Yesterday, Heather found a social media post from a relative she grew up with and loves dearly. He has struggled for years with drug addiction. He posted this statement which he had found on the internet to give us a perspective of what he and millions of others are going through:

> "So, everybody has their own opinions on drug and alcohol addiction, but until you've been there or had a family member there, your opinion remains insignificant. Yes, they chose to abuse a drug or alcohol thinking they would be one that would be able to control it. You don't control a drug or alcohol, it controls you. There are some lucky ones who have beat it, but don't think because they're still alive that life is gravy. They fight everyday all day to stay clean and sober. It's a constant battle from the time they

open their eyes until they close them, and it never goes away. Most are good people who made a bad choice. Battling a drug or alcohol addiction is a beast for the person addicted and the ones who love them...Drug and alcohol addiction is the abyss. Lost morals and lost souls. We all have demons!"[7]

This post really hit home. It is a graphic description to consider addiction an *abyss* that consumes lost souls - a graphic picture of this terrible life reality. This is the life he deals with every day and he understands that even if he is clean of the drugs in his system, the struggle will still remain. It also serves as a powerful, physical picture of the devastation even our most subtle inward sins can wreak so long as we, as believers, refuse to recognize that sin is no longer our master and yield to it. By yielding, or offering ourselves to sin, it gains control. However, once we *know* (chapter 4) we are dead to sin and raised with our all-powerful Savior, and we take the time to *consider* (chapter 5) what it would look like to be dead to sin but alive to God, we are nearly to the place of finding freedom from sin. But in order to fully enjoy this freedom, we must *offer* ourselves to God instead of to sin. Paul explains this in Romans 6:12-14:

> "Therefore, do not let sin reign in your mortal body so that you obey its evil desires. Do not offer any part of yourself to sin as an instrument of wickedness, but rather offer yourselves to God as those who have been brought from death to life; and offer every part of yourself to him as an instrument of righteousness. For sin shall no longer be your master, because you are not under the law, but under grace."

The pleasures of sin are short lived. Its reward lasts only

until the desire for that sin rises all over again within us. Its appetite is insatiable, never getting enough. Whether it be drugs, sex, alcohol, greed, hatred, bigotry or any other sin we offer ourselves to, there will never be enough to satisfy. I have never heard an alcoholic say to me, "I think I've had my fill. I'm tired of the hangovers." Usually, as we continue to offer ourselves to sin, it offers less and less back to us in return, causing us to offer even more of ourselves in order to find the satisfaction we enjoyed at the beginning. The reward becomes elusive, much harder to find than when we first started down the path. Not only that, but as Heather's family member posted, we eventually lose control and that sin we fight against gains the upper hand. It demands total allegiance.

We are faced with a choice the moment we are tempted to sin. There are two possible responses and the outcome is determined by the one to whom we choose to offer ourselves. The easiest and most popular response is to give in to sin. Ultimately, there is no place for sin to dominate our lives as Christians. Our hope is in the second response of believing God's word and realizing that the battle isn't really ours. We are instructed to, "offer yourselves to God..." (verse 13). In this verse, the word translated as "offer" or "present" is the Greek word "parastemi", which means "to yield."[8] Our old self, who we were before meeting Christ, offered or yielded its members to sin. We can all testify to this truth.

But, in true Christian form, we read in these verses that we have been "brought from death to life..." It is possible for the one who has trusted Christ to be delivered from the abyss of death, to find freedom in life. We now have the opportunity to "offer ourselves to God." Imagine, just as you once yielded yourself to the sin that was destroying you, you are now able to offer yourself to the One who gives life. As you once presented yourself to a tyrant who had no concern for you whatsoever, you are now able to offer yourself to the One who loved you to the very last measure of His life. Just as you offered yourself to destruction, now you have the wonderful opportunity to present yourself to the One who can put the broken pieces of your life back together. You were once dead in sin, now you can offer yourself to God as one who is alive and living for Him. You have been brought from death to life and the reward, through faith, is freedom from the sin that has kept you under its control for so long.

Not many of us have come back from the brink of death through the use of drugs or alcohol, but we have all been wounded--some so deeply that we can't express the pain of those wounds even to those nearest and dearest to us. We are all broken people. But God has been there the whole time. He is waiting for the moment when you are finally ready and willing to turn away from your sin, offer yourself to Him and experience freedom from the pain that sin and separation from God have left behind. He is waiting to see your form appear on the horizon so that He can run to embrace you.

The Offering

What a wonderful privilege to give ourselves completely, each member of our bodies, to the One to whom they already actually belong. That is what brings Him the most glory, when we realize the simple truth that we are not our own and willingly acknowledge that fact as we present ourselves entirely to Him. This wonderful privilege of presenting ourselves to God is the final stage in the process of our sanctification. This is the moment to savor that delicacy prepared for you, but the beauty of this moment is that it is shared with the One who has made it all possible. Think of it as a sacred meeting with God; the climax of a break-through in your relationship with Him.

Paul speaks about "presenting" ourselves to God later on in the book of Romans in chapter 12:1-2, which says,

"Therefore, I urge you, brothers and sisters, in view of God's mercy, to *offer your bodies* as a living sacrifice, holy and pleasing to God—this is your true and proper worship. Do not conform to the pattern of this world, but be transformed by the renewing of your mind. Then you will be able to test and approve what God's will is—his good, pleasing and perfect will" (emphasis added).

This passage occurs toward the end of the book of Romans as Paul sums up his theological teaching and begins to speak of practical ways of living. In essence, he is saying, "Because these things are true about God and about you, this is how you ought to live!"

Paul writes that, on the basis of God's mercy, we are to offer or present (parastemi) our bodies as a living and holy sacrifice. We are to place ourselves on the altar. Have you ever thought of yourself as being a sacrifice? In the worship practiced in the Old Testament, a sacrifice usually meant offering the entire animal. Paul uses the image of a sacrifice to paint a picture of complete surrender and because of God's mercy toward us, our only reasonable response is to place ourselves on the altar and to yield ourselves completely to Him because He, in His mercy, completely gave Himself for us on the cross.

Notice this is a voluntary act of worship. He has freed us from the power of sin and has given us purpose in life. There is no greater privilege than to serve and worship the King of kings by offering ourselves to Him; an offering He is fully worthy to receive. The essence of worship, after all, is our acknowledgement and consent of returning to Him what is rightfully His in the first place.

How do we "offer" ourselves in a significant and meaningful way? In keeping with the idea of worship, plan a time to be alone with God and - with sincere, heartfelt, and worshipful prayer -

present the members of your body to Him. Make it a solemn time just between the two of you. Ask Him to take what you have and offer it as a living sacrifice. Here are some examples:

Offer your hands for Him to use for His work.
Offer your feet to go where He leads you to go.
Offer your heart to love Him and those He loves.
Offer your arms to hold those who need to be comforted.
Offer your eyes to see those who are lost and in need.
Offer your ears to listen to those who are hurting and lonely.
Offer your mouth to speak His truth in love.
Offer your mind—that you may be transformed!

This is just between you and God, so make it as honest and personally applicable as you can. Take your time thinking through areas of challenge and reflect on how they should be transformed from a problem to a solution (a tongue that insults to one that encourages). When you do this, you will notice something happen that may surprise you. As you offer every part of yourself to righteousness, you will begin to notice that your focus will change from a self-centered perspective to a God-centered perspective. The true essence of worship is when He is given the central place of our lives.

The beautiful thing is that you can be sure God accepts your offerings. It delights His heart when one of His children yields every part of themselves to Him. It is the purest form of worship we can offer.

When you are done, write the date in your Bible next to these verses as the day you chose to "offer" yourself to the Lord as a complete sacrifice to Him. Then, when you face the temptation to sin, you can point to the day you offered your members to God to be used for His glory. Mark this day as a sign-post of your walk of faith. Allow it to be a continual reminder to you of who you are; a precious possession and valuable vessel of God. You are one who has willingly surrendered all that you are for His glory.

How will this impact you? It is as though you are offering Him the title to your life. You are giving to Him what is rightfully His to begin with – ownership of your entire body and all the resources and giftedness he has given to you. As a Christian, you have been redeemed, purchased, by the Savior. That redemption involves not only your spirit, but your body as well. By offering yourself to Him, you place your life, the life you are living today, in His hands from this time forward. You are setting yourself apart for Him in a way that so few ever do. As He receives that offering, you are recreating the sacrifice made by Jesus as He gave His whole body on the cross which was a sacrifice well pleasing to God (Ephesians 5:2).

Paul concludes this section back in Romans 6 by saying, "For sin shall no longer be your master, because you are not under the law, but under grace" (verse 14). This is such an important point; it is as though he were saying, "Stop behaving as someone who is still under the law where sin is your master and start living as someone who is free to live under the highest, greatest privilege of grace. Stop living as a beggar, start living as a child of the King." There certainly is no life that can compare to one lived in the freedom of grace. Why would we live in a prison of sin's power when we can live free in the palace of His grace? The life of grace is not only possible, but it is available to those who have trusted Jesus as their Savior and there is no better way to live. Nothing else can even begin to compare.

This is not Couch Potato Christianity

As we come to know, consider, and present or offer ourselves to God, it is important that this doesn't become a formula that you follow each time you sin. Pure and simple, this is about your *relationship* with the Lord Jesus. In the beginning of our walk with Him, we experience many mountain peaks and valleys. But as time goes on and these principles are applied, we find a more level ground as we mature in our relationship with Him. That doesn't mean that we won't have the peaks and valleys, but these principles have a stabilizing effect in our lives as we struggle with sin and our sinful nature.

Quite honestly, many criticize this way of thinking because they claim that we who believe in grace place all the responsibility for our sanctification on God and assume none ourselves. That is far from the truth. The bottom line is that we have to put effort into our relationship with Him. It is through our relationship with Him that grace is given and the struggle is won (2 Peter 1:3). Like any relationship, you must invest yourself into it for it to grow. There are no shortcuts. This is not couch potato Christianity, it is intentional. Granted, these principles are passive in nature as we place faith in what He has said, obey His word and rest in His power to overcome sin. However, we are responsible to turn from sin, confess when we have failed and pursue a holy life. The difference is realizing the power to overcome sin is His to provide, not mine.

It is all about relationship. I have seen in my own life that I must spend time with Him in His word and in prayer - it has become a necessity to me. That doesn't mean that if I miss a day in the word or have little time to pray that I have fallen from His grace. These things are not a measure of how good or bad of a Christian I am, but I must spend time with Him to understand His view of the world, the way He thinks and what it is that captures His heart. I want to know Him, to discover the depths of His great grace and my part in His ever-expanding Kingdom. Could there be anything more exciting or satisfying than to discover the heart of the Savior and to understand His love, mercy and grace?

Savoring the Delicacy

Try to think of your relationship with Jesus as the most treasured possession you have because, as His follower, that is exactly what it is. Your knowing, considering and presenting are to be an extension of that relationship, needed in order to maintain that most precious possession. Lay aside your rights as you give to Him, day by day, His rightful place. It is a daily commitment to die to yourself, to take up His cross and to give yourself to His purposes. It is an attitude of the heart, a choice and commitment to follow as He leads and obey as He directs. By applying these truths in your life, you have opened the door to a fuller relationship than you have ever imagined before. It is not a formula; it is faith in His design of how we handle the sin in our lives. You can now begin to savor the delicacy of your relationship with Jesus.

It is also a good idea to bring someone else into your struggle - someone who loves you and would be willing to check in on you (James 5:16). As we will discuss in the next chapter, we need one another and there could not be a more loving expression than to come alongside each other for the support we need to move beyond our struggle with sin.

Paul concludes his thoughts in Romans 6 by saying in verse 22, "But now that you have been set free from sin and have become slaves of God, the benefit you reap leads to holiness, and the result is eternal life." We will not be free from the *presence* of sin until the day we step into God's presence. However, we are already free from the *power* of sin by knowing that we were crucified and raised with Jesus, considering ourselves to be dead to sin but alive to God and offering the members of our body to God for His purposes. Through these principles, you will experience victory over sin in a very real and practical way.

Chapter six discussion questions.

1. What comes to mind as you think of what it means to "present" yourself to someone or something? What are the implications of such an act?

2. Discuss how the presenting of ourselves to God is an act of worship. What are we saying to Him when we present each member of our body to Him?

3. What is required as we are faced with a temptation to sin after we have presented the members of our body to God for His purposes? (Hint: this is much more than just writing a date in the margins of your Bible).

4. What do you notice about the progression of knowing, considering and presenting? What is absent when you consider that God directs you to apply these principles in your struggle against sin, regardless of how much of a hold that sin may have on your life?

Section Three – Incarnating Grace (chapters 7-12)

There is a well-kept secret, hidden in the pages of scripture but revealed throughout all of the Bible if one will see it. It is subtle but becomes obvious when brought to the attention of someone who is in relationship with the Lord Jesus. This secret has the potential to transform a life once the Spirit of God begins to apply this truth to the one open to receive it. This last section is intended to help navigate through some of our biggest obstacles-turned-opportunities if we are willing to allow the Spirit to lead us through them. This secret of incarnating grace can be understood in a single word – "Remain," which, at its core, has to do with surrender.

CHAPTER 7 – REMAINING IN THE VINE

John 15:4
*"Remain in me, as I also remain in you. No branch can bear fruit by itself;
it must remain in the vine. Neither can you bear fruit unless you remain in
me."*

A few years ago, I wanted to add some vegetation to our
backyard so on a trip to my hometown of Alamosa, in Southern
Colorado, I dug up a couple of aspen trees from the garden of my
brother-in-law's grandfather. The trees had overtaken that garden
plot, which should have been my first clue that this might not be
the wisest choice of tree to transplant. However, as a Colorado
native, I couldn't resist the tree that defines our state. Besides,
they were free!

I planted our two trees, which were about 6 feet tall, next
to the fence which we share with one of our neighbors. I was
excited with how well they grew. After a couple of years, it
seemed they had doubled in size. What I didn't realize is that they
were growing in more than just the obvious "upward" direction.
They were also growing outward, from underneath.

Aspen groves are considered to be some of the largest living
organisms on earth. It is thought that a single grove in Utah covers
over 106 acres of land and weighs as much as 14 million pounds.
All of those trees have grown off the root of a single tree.[9] I didn't
know this at the time, but it is a fact that I have come to appreciate.

Since the time I planted them, my two original aspen trees
have died, but between my neighbors (plural) and I, there are at
least 30 offspring that have replaced them. They grow
everywhere. I once found an aspen root growing next to my deck
and was horrified to see a dozen little trees underneath, growing
in the sunlight that made it down between the boards!

The thing I love most about my tree experience is seeing how well they thrive. Given the chance, those trees would grow in every direction, overcoming any and every obstacle their roots may encounter. The notable thing is that they grow together coming off the main root sent out from the original tree. From there, they send up shoots that reach for daylight sun and, before you know it, you have your own personal aspen grove.

This is the Colorado version of the principle that Jesus was getting at in John 15:1-17. He was speaking to His disciples and said that He was the Vine from which the branches, His followers, would grow and bear fruit. That is His design for you and me; to grow and bear fruit in our lives by being attached to Him, the Vine.

Even beyond that, His design is that we thrive in our relationship with Him which is actually the means by which that amazing fruit is produced. The way this happens is really remarkable. The sap we receive from the Vine is the divine strength and resource we must have to produce fruit. But, here is a very important point that we can't miss: just as a branch cut from a vine can produce no fruit, neither can we unless we stay attached, or remain, in the Vine. The natural response of branches is to remain attached, even though we may choose not to remain and miss out on one of the greatest blessings we could hope to experience. We may miss out on the very purpose for which we were created.

The Players - John 15:1-3

"I am the true vine, and my Father is the gardener. He cuts off every branch in me that bears no fruit, while every branch that does bear fruit, he prunes so that it will be even more fruitful. You are already clean because of the word I have spoken to you."

By studying the relationship between the vine and its branches, we can better understand the nature, motivation, and intimacy of our relationship with Jesus. We will be looking at these three aspects of our relationship with Him in this chapter. Jesus begins by identifying the key players in this relationship; Himself as the Vine, the Father as the gardener and His people as the branches.

Jesus begins by saying that the Father "cuts off" every branch that does not bear fruit (verse two). This could mean one of two things, either the Father sorts out those who truly don't know Jesus (an example would be Judas) or another use of the term "to cut off" in the Greek could mean, "to lift up." This lifting up could be to aid the branch in receiving more light and air which would help it to bear more fruit.[10]

To bear fruit, branches must occasionally be pruned. At times, the Father must prune those parts of our lives that hinder our relationship with Him. We will speak about this in the chapter concerning suffering. The process of pruning is often painful, but the results are amazing. I have seen trees completely cut down; however, within a year's time, branches have started growing right out of the stump. The same is true of those who have been pruned – having gone through that difficult process, they grow immensely in their faith and fruitfulness. A.W. Tozer once said, "It is doubtful whether God can bless a man greatly until He has hurt him deeply."[11] I have experienced the most growth when I've been faced with trials and suffering. The pruning is meant for our good, even though it hurts.

The Nature of the Relationship - The Vine and the Branches - John 15:4-8

"Remain in me, as I also remain in you. No branch can bear fruit by itself; it must remain in the vine. Neither can you bear fruit unless you remain in me. I am the vine; you are the branches. If you remain in me and I in you, you will bear much fruit; apart from me you can do nothing. If you do not remain in me, you are like a branch that is thrown away and withers; such branches are picked up, thrown into the fire and burned. If you remain in me and my words remain in you, ask whatever you wish, and it will be done for you. This is to my Father's glory, that you bear much fruit, showing yourselves to be my disciples."

I can think of few things more refreshing than being around a new believer in Jesus. The reason for this is that they are so excited about what God has done in their lives. They understand the release from their sin and the wonder of God's forgiveness. They are a completely new creature. It is a fresh start, like "being born again." Isn't that the perfect description of a new Christian? They are living in the reality that "a new creation has come" (2 Corinthians 5:17).

Something else that I love about them is that they understand the necessity of the nature of their relationship with Jesus. Just as a child depends on his parents, their dependency on Him is something that they know in their "everyday" life. It isn't until we move beyond the infancy stage that we are in danger of taking over again. Most of us, myself included, can testify that once we think we have the Christian life "figured out," we lose our sense of dependence. It is at that point that the fruit begins to wither.

Jesus is the Vine. All that is necessary for our lives flows from Him, whether physical or spiritual. He is able to supply it all. So many times, I have led Bible studies or taught Sunday school and asked Him to enable me to encourage people. I have given sermons that I thought would move people to further obedience because I believed many Christians have little desire to live for

Christ. I have done a lot of things for God that were done with pure intentions and genuine concern, but did not flow out of a dependent reliance upon the Vine. As a result, very little, if any, fruit was produced.

William MacDonald has said this, "Sometimes we pray, 'Lord, help me to live my life for you.' It would be better to pray, 'Lord Jesus, live out Your life through me.'"[12] That is the essence of remaining in the Vine. It is not what I can do for God but what He can do through me that matters. My part is to yield to Him which means that I give Him the freedom to do whatever it is He wants to do – to use me as He desires.

Jesus' Reliance on God

When we see ourselves as branches and Jesus as the Vine, it brings a new meaning to Jesus' teachings earlier in the book of John. Twice in the same chapter of John 5, Jesus tells his disciples that, "the Son can do nothing by himself; he can do only what he sees his Father doing, because whatever the Father does the Son also does" and later he says again, "By myself I can do nothing; I judge only as I hear, and my judgment is just, for I seek not to please myself but him who sent me" (John 5:19 and 30). Jesus recognized his own total and complete reliance as God the Son upon His Father. Jesus went so far as to say He could do "nothing" apart from the Father. That is amazing to me. God the Son was completely dependent on God the Father - Jesus as almighty God submitted to His Father and in the process, gave us the perfect example to follow as we submit ourselves to Him.

Jesus' reliance upon His Father during His earthly ministry is a vivid picture of our reliance upon Him, by His Spirit, through our earthly journey. If Jesus, as God the Son, was completely reliant upon His Father to the point He could do nothing apart from Him, how much more reliant would that make us upon Jesus? It was through Jesus' relationship to the Father that He was enabled to do all that He did, and it is our relationship with Jesus that enables us to bear fruit for Him that has any meaning or lasting value. Just like Jesus, we are to yield ourselves to the purposes of the Vine in order to bear the fruit He desires to produce in our lives. He then gives His divine strength and ability to bear that fruit, just as a vine provides all that is needed to its branches.

Yielding to Him doesn't mean that I do nothing at all or that I have no responsibility to God or others. What it does mean is that I look for what *He* is doing in my life and respond to His leading in faith. Each of us is uniquely placed in the lives of people around us. He has created each one of us with spiritual gifts and personality traits that enable us to minister to others.

Understanding the nature of our relationship to Jesus – He as the Vine and we as the branches – is essential when we think of bearing spiritual fruit in our lives. Who has He placed in your life that you are able to influence? Who, in that circle of influence, may He be asking you to speak with or to serve? He is the central Figure of life and without Him we can do nothing of lasting value. But, with Him, we can have a significant role in the lives of people around us.

Unfortunately, the opposite is also true. We may choose not to remain. In verse 6, Jesus is emphasizing the tragedy of not remaining in Him - the fruit withers and dies. It is good for nothing but to be thrown away and burned. Keep the context in mind that Jesus is talking about bearing fruit. This has nothing to do with losing our salvation. The tragedy is that there are many who bear no fruit and miss out on one of the greatest blessings as a believer. We can go all through our life and bear no fruit for what really matters. We may accumulate wealth or give ourselves to sports, recreation, social media or our jobs and miss out on those things that are eternal. None of those things are bad when kept in balance, but the point is that we don't want to miss our calling! How sad it will be on the day you stand before God to see that everything you lived for is nothing more than a pile of ash (1 Corinthians 3:10-15).

He must become Greater; I must become Less

John the Baptist was someone who understood this concept of remaining in the vine really well. He understood what it meant to "bear fruit" as the branch, as one who was completely dependent on the Vine. Before he was put into prison, John was told by some of his disciples of the numbers of people that had left him to follow Jesus. He was not angry or frustrated that so many had left, but he actually expressed joy that so many were now following Jesus because John knew he was not the Messiah but was instead a messenger sent ahead to prepare for the Messiah. Much like the best man at a wedding anticipates the arrival of the groom, John was overjoyed to realize that his role had been fulfilled because the groom had arrived. To these people he says, "He must become greater; I must become less" (John 3:30).

What a great reply! John got it - he understood his role as a branch. John's disciples, however, saw that the crowds were gone. John, they thought, a true servant of God had been left high and dry with little to show for his sacrifice and service. But because John understood his place as the branch, he was satisfied to be the "friend" who had the privilege of simply hearing the voice of the Savior which filled him with joy. He knew his mission was complete as the person who was to prepare hearts for the coming Savior. And, having understood these things and seeing Jesus begin His ministry, this humble servant accepted what many Christians in this "numbers-driven" world today would consider a loser's motto, "He must become greater, I must become less."

John understood a principle that is also essential in the Christian walk; Jesus comes first! As we mature in our walk with Him, we will begin to understand that this life isn't about us and what we can get out of it. The thing that really matters is what

Jesus can do through us. After all, the things we live to accumulate have a shelf-life; the things that we do for Jesus will last forever.

John understood this. He put Jesus ahead of everything else because he knew that true life flows from the Vine. The branch receives what it needs only from the Vine. But in practical terms, how do I remain in the Vine to receive what I need from it? How do I begin to live a life that is dependent on the Vine to produce fruit that will last into eternity? The answer: through faith.

Abiding Faith

Until I believe what God has said in His word, I will be detached from the Vine instead of remaining in it. It is a matter of believing who I am in Christ and trusting that He has created me for a purpose! Jesus said in John 15:7, "If you remain in me and my words remain in you, ask whatever you wish, and it will be done for you." How do His words remain in us?

First, we have to know what He said, which is what makes reading and meditating on the Bible absolutely essential. The Bible is the means through which He has chosen to reveal Himself to us and is essential in developing and deepening our relationship with Him. Like any relationship, we build it through the time we are willing to spend with that person and the same is true of our relationship with Jesus. Dedicate a part of each day to fully engaging your mind as you read and pray. Ask the Spirit to reveal the Savior to you. We grow in faith by believing that what He said is true (Romans 10:17). He will reveal His purpose for you. From there, you will find abundant and oftentimes, unexpected fruitfulness.

Bearing Fruit

Second, we are to look for the opportunities that the Father will open up to us. When Jesus said that whatever we wish will be done for us, He was speaking of the fruit that we have the potential to produce. This opens up endless possibilities! Look at where He has placed you and, by faith, step out when those opportunities He gives to you begin to surface. The Spirit will lead and nudge you in the direction you should go. We need to be attentive to His leading and obedient when He directs us to do something. If you are open to it and aware of His leading, you will begin to incarnate grace more and more often in your daily life.

You can be the top executive of a huge corporation or a dishwasher in a small country diner, yet your influence reaches far beyond yourself when you "remain in the Vine." Whether you are a stay-at-home mom or a traveling salesman, God will open just-for-you opportunities to impact people around you. Just like those aspen trees growing in my backyard, God has created you to thrive. And, after many years, even when you have gone home to be with Jesus, the growth of God's kingdom will continue because you, by faith, bore fruit that will last into eternity.

When we remain in Him and bear much fruit, the outcome brings great glory to the Father and "much fruit" in our lives that is proof that we are His disciples (John 15:8). It doesn't get much better than that. At the end of my life, I want others to see how God has used me as one of His disciples. I want to see my God glorified because I believed in Him enough to impact the lives of those around me. I hope to impact those lives because I yielded my life to Jesus to live His life through me. I pray that my greatest legacy would be His incarnated grace lived through me to a world that so desperately needs it. If that doesn't lift us to a higher purpose, I don't know what will.

The Motivation of our Relationship – Obedience through Love - John 15:9-11

"As the Father has loved me, so have I loved you. Now remain in my love. If you keep my commands, you will remain in my love, just as I have kept my Father's commands and remain in his love. I have told you this so that my joy may be in you and that your joy may be complete."

There is a direct connection between the love we have for God and our willingness to obey Him. We can attempt to follow God's commandments out of a legalistic attempt to earn His favor or out of obligation or guilt. However, when we are motivated by love, we will naturally want to follow His commands because we want to please the One we love.

Love is the great motivator. It willingly sacrifices its own rights for the object of its affection. It moves people to do some truly extraordinary things. Take, for example, Corporal Jason Dunham. During the Iraqi War, this 22-year-old Marine on April 14, 2004, fell on a grenade after getting in a scuffle with an Iraqi insurgent who dropped it intending to kill a group of Marines nearby. Dunham shielded them by using his helmet and body, saving the lives of at least two fellow Marines. He was awarded the Medal of Honor, posthumously, for his sacrifice.

This young man displayed the greatest act of love for his fellow Marines by placing himself in harm's way. Try to place yourself in the boots of those Marines who were saved by his heroic act. "He knew what he was doing. He wanted to save Marines' lives from that grenade," said Lance Cpl. Jason Sanders.[13] Such as sacrifice will mark forever those Jason saved by his death.

We, as followers of the Lord Jesus Christ, find ourselves in these same boots. Jesus died for us and His sacrifice saved us from eternal death. His great love, displayed on the cross, ought to motivate us to love Him in return. The best way to express that love is to honor Him by following His commands. This love should motivate us to live each day of our lives for Him.

Obedience motivated by love is the direct result of simply

remaining in the Vine. It is so true that we honor the Savior for His sacrifice; that is exactly what we should do. For most of us, that is where we begin in our relationship with Him. We understood that He died for us and we responded in love and gratitude for what He has done. However, as the relationship with Him deepens, I realize that there is so much more to the Savior's love. I begin to understand Him as a person and to appreciate new insights about Him. I not only read about His interactions with people in the Bible, but I begin to see Him working in my own life. Even those difficult circumstances I encounter through the course of the day become opportunities to tap deeper into "the Vine." As He gives me the divine strength to face those circumstances, love naturally flows back to the Vine from that living, breathing relationship that I have with Him. My obedience is the result of my deeper relationship that is produced by remaining in the Vine.

There is a wonderful benefit to obeying Jesus. It was something that John the Baptist spoke about when he said that his joy was "now complete" after realizing he had finished the task he was sent to do. Jesus gives you His joy when you obey Him (verse 11). There is something about the joy you experience when realizing it came as a direct result of obeying your God even in the smallest way. Perhaps it's the understanding that you are a part of a huge plan that is unfolding as God's kingdom grows by the obedience of His people. Perhaps it's like a child that knows he is standing in the glow of his parents' unconditional love. Even during the hardest of circumstances or the darkest of days, joy can carry you through because it isn't based on what happens to you, but rather, on an inner peace and satisfaction that you truly are standing in the glow of our Savior's unconditional love.

The Intimacy of our Relationship - The Incarnation of Jesus' Love - John 15:12-17

Not only does remaining in the vine keep us in relationship

with our Lord, but it also puts us in proper relationship with one another. The Lord spoke of the intimacy of our relationships in John 15:12-17 on the horizontal plane with each other as well as the vertical plane with Himself.

> "My command is this: Love each other as I have loved you. Greater love has no one than this: to lay down one's life for one's friends. You are my friends if you do what I command. I no longer call you servants, because a servant does not know his master's business. Instead, I have called you friends, for everything that I learned from my Father I have made known to you. You did not choose me, but I chose you and appointed you so that you might go and bear fruit—fruit that will last—and so that whatever you ask in my name the Father will give you. This is my command: Love each other."

The one resounding commandment of our Savior was that His followers love one another. From personal experience, this can be the hardest commandment to obey. We are all broken people in so many ways – I can't even begin to count my own frailties. When you put a bunch of broken people together, you never know what will happen. One moment can be explosive, and the next, you may witness the deepest expressions of love you would ever hope to see.

Some of my fondest memories, as well as deepest wounds, have come from brothers and sisters in the church. I have often thought that I would love to give myself more fully to God's people and yet fear to show any vulnerability because of the times I've been hurt. To say the least, to love one another can be complicated. What complicates things even more is *how* we are to love one another – as Jesus has loved us.

He tells his disciples, "Greater love has no one than this: to lay down one's life for one's friends" (John 15:13). Talk about vulnerability. No one has been more vulnerable than a holy God incarnate allowing sin-filled men to kill Him to show us the extent of His love. If He could do that, how is it that I can't give myself to His people? How is it that I can't be vulnerable enough to accept and love you as my brother or sister in Christ?

Now, He lives to bring you into relationship, not only with Himself, but with all those who make up the family of God. We who are family are commanded to love one another. The fact that He said this the night before His crucifixion shows that he waited until just before He suffered to drive home the point. After all, a lot is riding on this command. Our very witness as His disciples is seen by this dying and hateful world because of our love for one another (John 13:35). Our actions, in this case, speak much louder than our words.

However, we need to make this very practical. We're in this together; branches that are living off the same Vine. Sharing the same life source means that we remain in Him together. Whether we are willing to admit it or not, we need each other. We can't survive without one another. Cut off one branch from the rest and it will wither. Jesus knew this which is why He gave us this command to love one another. This is a huge part of remaining in the Vine. This is where the rubber meets the road. This is where incarnating grace becomes practical. Let's face it, incarnating His love (loving as He loved) is hard, so I wanted to commit a large portion of the book to addressing what incarnating grace looks like on a practical level. There is, perhaps, no greater challenge to the human heart than to incarnate the love of Jesus which is exactly why we need His incarnating grace to accomplish it.

From here, we will examine how this essential aspect of remaining in the Vine literally affects every part of our lives. We will look at quite a few facets of our living. There are so many things that can hinder us from maintaining relationships with one another - keeping us from remaining in the Vine. It is so important to consider what may cause us to detach from the Vine. But, before then, I just want to leave you with one more thought concerning the most important relationship we have: our friendship with Jesus.

Face to Face

Jesus said in this passage that we are His friends if we follow His commandment to love. Your friendship with Jesus was something He had in mind even before the world began! Paul tells the Ephesians that God "chose us in him before the creation of the world..." Before any of this began, you were in the mind of God – chosen by Him to have a relationship with Him. What kind of worth does that place on you as one chosen by God before He created anyone or anything? What value do you have in His eyes? You have more worth to Him than you will ever know.

It is too far beyond any of us to fully grasp this wonderful truth. Just imagine His anticipation for the day that you were born. I think it filled His heart with joy to know that finally, you who are so precious to Him, had arrived on the scene. Imagine the joy that filled the heart of Jesus when you, His friend, first placed your trust in Him. Imagine how, unknown to you, He has laughed with you and cried with you as He led you through all of your life's celebrations and trials. Finally, imagine His joy when, on the day you die, He will finally see you face to face, revealed to you as the best friend you have ever had! Build into that relationship today as you abide in the Vine.

Chapter seven discussion questions.

1. Do you think Jesus' reliance upon His Father reveals a weakness on His part? Why would He fall into such dependence upon God? How does Jesus' total and complete reliance upon His Father translate into our total and complete reliance upon Him?

2. Discuss why faith in God's word concerning who we are in Christ is essential to remaining in the Vine.

3. Why is love the only true, legitimate motivation for obeying God? If our obedience is for any other reason, what does that say of our perception of God?

4. How can we live in the reality that Jesus is our friend? Does it stir up uneasy feelings in you to think of Him as a friend? If so, why is that? What does it mean to you, personally, that He actively works in our lives and waits for our eventual meeting, face to face?

CHAPTER 8 – THE PERFORMANCE TRAP

Galatians 5:1
"It is for freedom that Christ has set us free. Stand firm, then, and do not let yourselves be burdened again by a yoke of slavery."

In 1994, Heather and I were living in Tallinn, the capital city of Estonia in Eastern Europe, doing missions work. Every night while we slept, a reliable passenger ferry called the *MV Estonia* crossed the Baltic Sea full of passengers and vehicles heading for Stockholm, Sweden.

However, on September 28, we awoke on a cold and windy morning to discover that the Estonia had never made it to her destination. She had sunk to the bottom of the Baltic Sea during the night.

The ship was a "roll on/roll off" ferry, so called because a visor serving as a bow could be lifted while at dock to allow vehicles to "roll on" or drive into the ship and lowered to serve as a bow while at sea. Once at their destination the vehicles would "roll off" or disembark through the other end of the ship.

An investigation of the wreck was conducted and testimony from survivors revealed a metallic "bang" sound at 12:55 a.m. which is believed to have been hinges detaching from the hull. The locking devices, hinges and lifting cylinder mountings that held the visor on the ship were literally torn off the hull by the waves produced by a heavy storm, causing it to tumble forward and eventually drop off the ship completely. This, in turn, allowed water to enter the vehicle deck and, in less than an hour, the ship listed completely to one side before sinking to the bottom of the Baltic.[14]

In comparison to the enormity of the ship, those hinges and locks were a very small part of the whole. Yet, their failure was key to the worst maritime disaster to have occurred during peacetime on the Baltic. We saw the effects on the people of Estonia in the following days as this small nation mourned their losses.

Shipwrecked Faith

It doesn't take much to shipwreck the faith of believers. Just as those hinges served a vital purpose, we need to understand that the very things that seem to be inconsequential may have a serious impact on our own life and the lives of others. We must beware of the subtle ways in which our faith can be shipwrecked. They may be as subtle as preferences or insecurities we bring to our beliefs outside the teaching of Scripture.

The Bible records an example of how the early church could potentially have been shipwrecked. Were it not for one leader who confronted the rest, the church could have potentially capsized, wrecking the faith of many and causing a rift that could have existed even today.

A Shaken Pillar

In Galatians 2:11-14, the Apostle Paul records a confrontation he had with Peter, a pillar of the church:

"When Cephas (Peter) came to Antioch, I opposed him to his face, because he stood condemned. For before certain men came from James, he used to eat with the Gentiles. But when they arrived, he began to draw back and separated himself from the Gentiles because he was afraid of those who belonged to the circumcision group. The other Jews joined him in his hypocrisy, so that by their hypocrisy even Barnabas was led astray. When I saw that they were not acting in line with the truth of the gospel, I said to Cephas in front of them all, "You are a Jew, yet you live like a

Gentile and not like a Jew. How is it, then, that you force Gentiles to follow Jewish customs?"

The church in Antioch was composed of both Jews and non-Jews or Gentiles. Peter and Paul were ministering there when some Jewish believers from the church in Jerusalem (where James was a leader) arrived unexpectedly. Up until this time, they had both been enjoying the company of the Gentile believers, including eating meals with them, without any hesitation.

At the arrival of those from Jerusalem, however, Peter felt guilty that he was going against Jewish tradition by allowing himself to be in the home of a Gentile and eating with them. As one raised as a Jew, he immediately began to pull away and separate himself from the Gentile believers. He feared his fellow Jews would not approve even though all present, Jews and Gentiles, were believers in the Lord Jesus. This is when Paul knew he had to confront Peter's behavior.

You have to admire the courage of Paul. Peter was a pillar in the church who had the ability to influence those around him and rightfully so; he walked with the Lord Jesus through all His ministry and led the church from its infancy. To have confronted Peter, to his face, in front of everyone else would have been tremendously difficult. Yet, Paul knew that Peter was dead wrong and too much was at stake if such an influential leader was making such a terrible mistake. Peter demonstrated that even those who know better may fall victim to "performance-based acceptance" or "the performance trap.

Peter suffered from the same sin as so many, including myself. He had a fear of man, or put a different way, a fear of disappointing others. Before the arrival of these Jewish men, Peter had no problem dining with the Gentile believers—something which would have been unthinkable before his conversion to Christ. But Peter knew better. He was the first of the apostles to share the gospel with the Gentiles. We read about this in Acts 10 when the Lord sent him to the Roman Centurion, Cornelius. It was at this time when, in a vision, God told Peter that he should not consider the Gentiles to be "unclean." Peter was faithful to present the gospel and, to his surprise, they believed the message and received the Savior.

Peter's fear in Antioch of these Jewish men may have come from what happened as a result of his going to the home of Cornelius. We read in Acts 11:2-3, "So when Peter went up to Jerusalem, the circumcised (Jewish) believers criticized him and said, "You went into the house of uncircumcised men and ate with them." Their questioning of Peter may have been enough to cause him to second guess himself and to fear the response of those who came from Jerusalem to Antioch years later.

Regardless, Paul confronted Peter to his face. This was especially important because others, including a mature believer like Barnabas, were also carried away in the hypocrisy. For Peter to commit this sin and go without rebuke led many others under his influence down the same road of hypocrisy, pride and ultimately, legalism. This would have led to a fall and shipwreck of the faith of many believers, making a division between those who were Jews and those who were Gentiles. It's amazing how such a small thing such as the unwillingness to eat with Gentile believers could cause such problems. Peter's example could have produced a division that should never be seen in the church (Galatians 3:28). Peter's desire to be accepted by the Jews showed a weakness in his faith; he wanted to *perform* well in order to gain their acceptance.

A Church in Fear

Performance-based acceptance has a way of leading to a strict form of legalism. If we are out of balance in our efforts to impress others with how well we perform as Christians, we may set ourselves up to be more concerned with receiving acceptance from them than we are with simply following our Savior. In other words, an indication that we are out of balance is when we are more concerned with what others think about us than we are in pleasing Jesus. When this happens, every behavior may be scrutinized by someone as to whether it is the "Christian" thing to do. This is where legalism may come into the picture.

Let me give you a modern-day example of how destructive a performance-based motivation leading to legalism can be to a church. Before we begin, perhaps we should define a legalist. This is someone who places others under obligation to follow a list of what they, themselves, see as living righteously before God. Usually, they justify their actions by going beyond the bounds of Scripture or twist what the Scriptures say into what they want it to mean. They often base their law on a preference or conviction they feel strongly about, then manipulate others into obedience by giving them their set of rules to live by.

A couple we knew at a church we formerly attended have a daughter who married a young man she met while attending Bible college. Certain family members of this young husband were in leadership of the church they attended. As a result of a theological disagreement between the leadership of the church and the parents of the wife, this young couple were instructed to break their relationship with her parents. As a result, our friends have lost all contact with their daughter and grandchildren.

The reason for this separation is based on a belief the leadership of this church adheres to. It is believed that to maintain unity in the church, all who attend must be blameless. One of the leaders in the church, known as "the arbitrator," decides whether or not people in the church are blameless. It has progressed to the point that he inspects the closets of young women or girls of the church to assess whether or not their clothing is "blameless." This is just one example of several actions he has taken to dominate the church. This leader has given himself total control and the church is to accept, without question, his conclusions whether they agree with them or not. Their role is simply to submit to his decisions.

A sense of fear permeates this church. Those who have succeeded in leaving have said that every behavior and even physical appearance is under constant scrutiny. All of this began some time earlier when this leader (the arbitrator) determined that the elders of the former church he and his family attended were not living blameless lives. He split the church, taking several families with him. He then took several steps beyond what Scripture says in order to justify his behavior and, in the process, capsized the spiritual lives of many people.

Several families who originally left with him later found themselves, for one reason or another, under church discipline which means they are shunned by the rest of the church and not allowed to attend church services any longer. They went from following this leader to finding themselves outside of his acceptance. Imagine the pressure of living under such scrutiny and then having failed to live up to the expectation of this one man, wrestling with feelings of guilt, thinking that they had failed Christ. After leaving, several families have been able to return to the original church they left when they followed him and have found some measure of healing in their lives.

In the face of such circumstances, the natural inclination of the typical new Christian is that should they fail to perform or live up to the expectations of the church leadership, they have failed God; that their "performance" in some way affects God's love and acceptance of them. Is it any wonder that so many Christians feel like failures when it comes to their relationship with Christ? Many are guilt-ridden and overwhelmed by their "sin" which is the tactic legalists use to keep them under their influence.

The Legalist's Tool

The performance trap is the greatest tool in the hand of a legalist. They mold people into their own image, being fully convinced that they are doing everyone, including God, a favor by living according to the law and forcing others to do the same. Many legalists willingly admit that they are saved by God's grace, but then, for some reason, feel obligated to revert back to the law in order to live righteously before Him. They teach this belief to others, who are then in danger of living their entire lives under obligation to the law rather than in the freedom and love of Christ. Many believers have suffered the shipwreck of their spiritual lives because of this fallacy.

To be perfectly honest, I have been on both the giving and receiving end of the performance trap. Early in my Christian experience, I felt obligated to lead and follow others with more concern for their acceptance of "how I was doing" rather than a genuine concern to do so out of a love for my Savior and other believers. It wasn't until my focus changed that I began to be released from this trap. Seeing myself as God sees me by gaining a clearer understanding of who I am in Christ brought balance to my life that allowed me to let go of the need for acceptance. That one small desire for acceptance by others had the potential to shipwreck my spiritual life (Galatians 1:10).

Finding the Anchor

As I just said, the way to combat this fallacy is to understand the fundamental truth of our identity with Christ. We again pick up Paul's argument against Peter in Galatians 2:19-20:

"For through the law I died to the law so that I might live for God. I have been crucified with Christ and I no longer live, but Christ lives in me. The life I live in the body I live by faith in the Son of God, who loved me and gave Himself for me."

By faith we understand that we have died to the law in order that we might live for God. As God sees it, we died when the Lord Jesus died. Now, we are free to allow the Lord Jesus to live His life in and through us, "and I no longer live, but Christ lives in me." By faith in the Lord Jesus, I accept this fact as true and give myself to Him to live His life through me. He becomes the anchor I need to keep me from the shipwreck of seeking the acceptance of others rather than simply receiving His acceptance of me.

Galatians 2:21 says,

"I do not set aside the grace of God, for if righteousness could be gained through the law, Christ died for nothing!"

We can't revert back to the law to somehow attain righteousness or gain God's acceptance. To say that our righteousness comes from any other source other than the cross would mean that our Savior died for no reason at all. We cannot stand in our own righteousness because we have none (Isaiah 64:6). Jesus' sacrifice fulfilled the requirements of the law for us and that is the reason why we must stand in His righteousness. As we see back in the book of Philippians, by faith, we will, "...be found in him, not having a righteousness of my own that comes from the law, but that which is through faith in Christ—the righteousness that comes from God on the basis of faith" (Philippians 3:9).

The Motive for Our Service

Grace stands alone. It stands apart from the Law. In it we get a glimpse of who God really is. He is so incredibly loving, so incredibly giving. Even though we deserve His wrath, He pours out His grace upon us. We stand before Him perfect because we stand before Him "in Christ." Because the Lord Jesus lives His life through us, we can't be any more acceptable to God or accepted by God. His great grace has brought us into His family as His children. A holy life is possible because *He* enables us to live it (2 Peter 1:2-3).

What all this means, particularly in regard to serving Him, is that I can stop attempting to meet someone else's "standards." I can stop doing what I or others think I should be doing so that I am free to do what Jesus wants me to do (1 Thessalonians 2:4, 1 Corinthians 4:3-4, Galatians 1:10). In this way, it becomes possible to live for Him, or as Paul says in Galatians 2:20, to allow Him to live His life through me because, "I no longer live, but Christ lives in me."

A legalist, on the other hand, will often emphasize the fear of God as a motive for godly living, even to the exclusion of His love. But, in complete contrast to the legalist, Jesus was completely motivated by His love. Again, Galatians 2:20 tells us that He, "loved me and gave Himself for me". The only natural response as the recipient of that kind of love is stated so simply in 1 John 4:19, "We love, because He first loved us." When you realize the depth of the love He has for you, you can't help but love Him in return and to place yourself in His service as His bond-servant. Service for Him now flows out of a heart of love, praise, gratitude and worship. Once you have this perspective, it is easy to follow His example in serving out of love. That kind of service is never a burden.

However, if we serve out of a sense of obligation or guilt, for example, we find ourselves eventually faced with exhaustion. The energy to serve tends to run out quickly because the Vine does not produce fruit through obligation or guilt - neither of which are listed as a fruit that the Vine does produce - love, joy, peace, forbearance, kindness, goodness, faithfulness, gentleness and self-control (Galatians 5:22-23).

Why am I Trying to Perform?

What took place with Peter may seem like a minor thing, but if Paul had not confronted Peter, the church may have divided because the Gentiles would never have had the same status as Jewish believers. This separation of the Gentiles and Jews would have been devastating. If the Lord had not led Paul to intervene, there could still be, even today, a divide between the two groups. The church would be even more fragmented than it already is. We need each other way too much for that to happen. Paul would assert his deep conviction for the unity of the church to the fullest measure by telling the Galatian believers later in this same letter, "There is neither *Jew nor Gentile*, neither slave nor free, nor is there male and female, for you are all one in Christ Jesus" (Galatians 3:28, emphasis added).

Are you attempting to "perform well" in order to gain the approval of God or man? Ask yourself what it is in your life that is contributing to this performance-based mentality? Granted, we are judged from childhood on how well we do or do not perform. We are rewarded for hard work as it relates to our performance in school or on the job. However, those ways of thinking could very well hinder your relationship with God if your motive is to seek His approval by your performance. It is impossible to abide in the Vine if you are in a constant state of worry, wondering if you have performed well enough to please Him each day. Instead, you can rest in Him knowing full well that He loves and accepts you just the way you are.

Beware the Legalist

As I look around, I realize there are many who would love to place others under their influence and control by manipulation. They desire to overpower others to get what they want and this mentality is clearly seen in the church today. Most churches are led by men who sincerely love God and are motivated by that love. Some, however, place the law as the gauge for measuring holiness, failing to understand that the law has already served its purpose in leading us to the Savior (Galatians 3:24).

But of all those I see, there is one I fear most, and I look him in the mirror each day. We all have the potential to fall under the control of someone or dominate those God has placed in our lives. We need to be very discerning and cautious to understand the dangers of getting out of balance either way - to beware the legalist inside of us. Because love is the motivation for our service, anything else, such as guilt, insecurity, or obligation, is not an acceptable motive. You cannot remain in the Vine and serve or force others to serve out of motivations that will eventually lead to exhaustion and the possible ruin of their spiritual lives.

By incarnating His grace, we are free to live for Christ out of *His* resources and to serve Him out of a heart of love, worship and gratitude for who He is and what He has done for us. When His grace is incarnated in us we do not live in fear that He will reject us if we fail to follow the laws of man. It is the love of Christ that controls us. My life's verse speaks about this,

> "For Christ's love compels us, because we are convinced that one died for all, and therefore all died. And he died for all, that those who live should no longer live for themselves but for him who died for them and was raised again" (2 Corinthians 5:14-15).

Once you have received His grace, there will be no going back because the freedom He gives is true freedom indeed (John 8:36). Once you have tasted that freedom, you will settle for nothing less.

Chapter eight discussion questions.

1. Discuss what you see is a reason we attempt to perform in order to win God's approval.

2. What role does the fear of man play in the life of someone caught in the performance trap? What is it that such a person fails to understand about God and our relationship with Him?

3. How is it that we have been released from the Law? What freedom do we find having been released from it? Does this mean we can live as we please?

4. If you are someone who attempts to perform for God or man's approval, what is it in your past that drives you to do this? What steps can you take to walk away from this bondage?

CHAPTER 9 – ACCEPTING THOSE UNLIKE US

Romans 15:7
"Accept one another, then, just as Christ accepted you, in order to bring praise to God."

Here's a story that illustrates the power of welcoming acceptance as told by Rebecca Manley Pippert:

"When I first came to Portland, Oregon, I met a student on one of the campuses where I worked. He was brilliant and looked like he was always pondering the esoteric. His hair was always mussy, and in the entire time I knew him, I never once saw him wear a pair of shoes. Rain, sleet or snow, Bill was always barefoot.

While he was attending college, he had become a Christian. At this time, a well-dressed, middle-class church across the street from the campus wanted to develop more of a ministry to the students. They were not sure how to go about it, but they tried to make them feel welcome.

One day Bill decided to worship there. He walked into this church, wearing his blue jeans, t-shirt and of course no shoes. People looked a bit uncomfortable, but no one said anything. So, Bill began walking down the aisle looking for a seat. The church was quite crowded that Sunday, so as he got down to the front pew and realized that there were no seats, he just squatted on the carpet - perfectly acceptable behavior at a college fellowship, but perhaps unnerving for a church congregation.

The tension in the air became so thick one could slice it. Suddenly an elderly man began walking down the aisle toward the boy. Was he going to scold Bill? My friends who saw him approaching said they thought, "You can't blame him. He'd never guess Bill is a Christian. And his world is too distant from Bill's to understand. You can't blame him for what he's going to do." As the man kept walking slowly down the aisle, the church became utterly silent, all eyes were focused on him, you could not hear anyone breathe. When the man reached Bill, with some difficulty he lowered himself and sat down next to him on the carpet. He and Bill worshiped together on the floor that Sunday."[15]

I know people, and I'm sure you do too, that are a lot like this old man. They so incarnate grace that they resemble the Lord Jesus as He is described in the book of John as One "full of grace." Their focus is always outward, and they go to great pains to express love to others. But what often happens is that we more resemble the congregation when someone different shows up in our lives. We become uptight and uncomfortable when someone doesn't meet our expectations of what we think a "Christian" or "believer" should be or even look like. It might be a difference of what they wear or, as has been one of my prejudices in the past, bodies full of tattoos. How quickly we come to conclusions about people we don't even know within seconds of encountering them.

Not only that, but like we discussed in the last chapter, we can get side-tracked on any given issue that is often a matter of personal conviction or preference. Those issues can range anywhere from Bible translations we use to how we school our children to whether we sing contemporary or traditional music in the church. Let's be clear, we are not to compromise the Word of God in the least. If it is in the Bible, it is black and white. However, what we need to understand is that if it is a "gray" issue, we can't make it black or white. We need to be careful not to force our list of gray issues on another or to judge our brother or sister who doesn't share our opinion.

What are Your Gray Issues?

As with any issue, we have two extremes when it comes to the matter of personal convictions. On the one side, you have those who are convinced that something is cut and dry, that this is the way it is and anyone who disagrees is either in sin or heading that way fast. Then you have the other extreme of those who are wondering what the big deal is and why anyone would struggle with something which, in their opinion, is so trivial. Their attitude is that they will enjoy their Christian liberty whether you like it or not and it is completely your problem if you don't!

Most of us tend to avoid extremes, but we all have those issues that we hold close, even closer than we may have imagined. Suddenly, and with no warning, our head nearly explodes when someone says something negative or opposed to the way we think.

We are going to look at a couple of Scriptures to see how the apostles handled a gray issue that emerged during the early days of the Christian church in order to see how this example can help us maintain a balance when it comes to handling our own set of gray issues and, most importantly, how we can incarnate grace to other believers regardless of where they stand.

In the early church there was a lot of discussion as to whether or not it was permissible to eat meat that was sacrificed to idols. Apparently, meat from these animals was sold in pagan temples and believers were confronted with whether or not they should eat it. On top of this, there were also dietary restrictions that came from Judaism that restricted Jewish believers from eating certain meats (Leviticus 11). It was a very divisive issue.

No Pork for Me, Thanks
Paul addresses this gray area head on, writing to the Corinthians:

"Now about food sacrificed to idols: We know that 'We all possess knowledge.' But knowledge puffs up while love builds up...So then, about eating food sacrificed to idols: We know that an idol is nothing at all in the world' and that 'There is no God but one'...yet for us there is but one God, the Father, from whom all things came and for whom we live; and there is but one Lord, Jesus Christ, through whom all things came and through whom we live" (1 Corinthians 8:1,4 and 6).

Paul sets the stage for the resolution of this issue even before getting to the issue itself. He is talking about knowledge and the fact that knowledge, if not mixed with love, becomes arrogance. Knowledge, by itself, attracts attention to self; a display of what we "know." Love, on the other hand, looks outside of self to the benefit of others. If we can grasp this, the issues we are discussing now would resolve themselves. But, for practical purposes, Paul fleshes out how the Corinthians were to deal with this issue. This gives us invaluable wisdom on how to deal with our own set of issues regarding personal preferences.

To begin with, Paul reminds the believers that the issue of the idol is not the main problem. There is but one God and our lives are created by and for Him. The idol is nothing because it is just that, an idol. It has no power over the believer. The issue has to do with the perception of how those who were not yet mature in their faith viewed the idol and what was sacrificed to it.

Let's consider, first of all, those who didn't think any Christian should eat the meat sacrificed to idols. Many were saved from pagan societies in which their temples were central to their entire existence. Think of how someone who served many deities was forced to appease those deities by making sacrifices to obtain what they wanted or needed from their gods. After becoming believers, they were set free from the terrible bondage of serving idols but must have struggled with eating from that sacrifice. By eating that meat, they would naturally feel that they are taking part, all over again, with the sacrifices they once felt they had to make in serving other gods. Considering their context, it is understandable that they believed eating these offerings would defile them.

Such a person's conclusion is that anyone who eats this meat is in sin. A parallel passage that also deals with eating meat sacrificed to idols is found in Romans 14. In this passage, Paul reminds believers that a brother or sister is free to refuse to eat the meat, but regardless he or she "must not judge the one who does (eat the meat), for God has accepted them. "Then Paul asks, "Who are you to judge someone else's servant? To their own master, servants stand or fall. And they will stand, for the Lord is able to make them stand" (Romans 14:3-4).

Pass the Pork Chops, Please

The other extreme on the spectrum of preferences is the person who feels it is safe to eat meat sacrificed to idols. He does not care what anyone else thinks. He is convinced that he has certain liberties in Christ and can't imagine how someone would live in fear of the idols like those who, in this case, refuse to eat this meat. The way he thinks about it is that Christ has set him free to partake as he pleases and can't understand why anyone would make such a big deal out of this. Besides, the meat sold at the local temple was a bargain and who wouldn't want that? Such people, in his not so humble opinion, need to lighten up.

Years ago, I was in charge of assigning men who would speak on Sunday mornings in a campground of a national park near my hometown. The church we were attending at the time had been granted permission by the Park Service to conduct Sunday morning services and we saw it as an opportunity to encourage travelers who were believers and to present the gospel to the lost.

It also gave opportunities for some of our younger guys to develop their skill of preaching.

I approached one brother who had been in the church for quite some time and seemed interested in sharing the gospel. He agreed and we went to the campground the following Sunday. The thing about this guy was that he had relatively long hair in an era when that was less acceptable in the church. We all knew that he had a genuine love for God and was a good husband and father, so it never occurred to me that his hair would be an issue.

Interestingly, it didn't seem to be an issue to those who were camping that weekend, either, but it was to him. He began his message by saying that long hair was a liberty he enjoyed in Christ and anyone who didn't like it was "welcome to leave." After picking my jaw up off the ground, I looked around to see if anyone was offended, but graciously, all stayed to hear his message. It is one thing to enjoy our liberties in Christ, but quite another to flaunt those freedoms or dare people to challenge you on them.

Paul's exhortation to this extreme is found in Romans 14:3, "The one who eats everything must not treat with contempt the one who does not." Another word used more often today for "contempt" would be "despise." We are not to despise someone who does not eat that meat. By doing so, we are showing no love to one who, for their conscience's sake, could not eat it. In the same way, that brother with the long hair should not have shown contempt, or despised, any Christian whom he thought would disagree with his long hair. We may know that we have the freedom to do such things, but if we look down on those who don't agree, our knowledge only puffs us up instead of building others up. Paul states the seriousness of the situation in 1 Corinthians 8:12, "When you sin against them in this way and wound their weak conscience, you sin against Christ."

The Lord takes offense when we despise others. He calls us to live lives that are constantly outwardly focused. How easy it is to judge one another or to despise those whom we see as weak in conscience. Any time a personal preference creates a division, God sees this as a sin against Christ. Paul wants us, as believers, to understand just how serious this is by reminding us that we all will be judged one day - both for our sinful behavior but also for showing contempt to others for their appearance or behavior. "You, then, why do you judge your brother or sister? Or why do you treat them with contempt? For we will all stand before God's judgment seat... So then, each of us will give an account of ourselves to God" (Romans 14:10, 12). How will we answer God for the times that we judged or despised those with whom we disagreed over something as small as a preference, as if it were a doctrine?

Our Preferences Today

Of the many issues that have surfaced in the church, there is one "hot topic" of our day that rivals the issue of meat sacrificed to idols in Paul's day. So much division has occurred in the church today over music played during worship. I know people who draw the line when it comes to the kind of music or instruments played in a church. They would refuse to fellowship in a church if the music were too contemporary or too traditional. By making such a distinction they have elevated their own opinion to the status of a doctrine and judge the church as spiritual or unspiritual based upon what they hear during the worship service. Some churches, recognizing this issue, now offer both options at different times so that the congregation can choose to attend their preference. And, whether we like it or not, this is an issue of preference. There are both good and bad songs and hymns from every era. The question should be the content of truth found in our songs and whether or not the song focuses our attention toward the One whom we worship.

The point is that extremes, no matter what they are, place us at polar ends. More than ever before, we need to find balance. I believe Paul knew the way to find that balance. His focus was on loving others, and he was so outward focused that he was willing to do without anything that would cause his brother or sister in Christ to stumble. Scripture gives us several examples of this wonderful expression of his love for fellow believers: "Therefore, if what I eat causes my brother or sister to fall into sin, I will never eat meat again, so that I will not cause them to fall" (1 Corinthians 8:13), and "It is better not to eat meat or drink wine or to do anything else that will cause your brother or sister to fall" (Romans 14:21).

The question we have to ask ourselves is whether or not we love our brothers and sisters in Christ enough that we are willing to sacrifice some of the liberties or preferences that we enjoy for their sake. As you consider those liberties, think of them in light of the worth of our brothers and sisters in Christ. Some issues we feel deeply about and may even cause our temperature to rise if we feel they are threatened. But, put them in perspective of this thought that Paul brings up in Romans 14:15, "If your brother or sister is distressed because of what you eat, you are no longer acting in love. Do not by your eating destroy someone for whom Christ died." Since our Savior valued that brother or sister enough to sacrifice His own life for them, shouldn't we be willing to sacrifice something as small as a preference or opinion for them? We must never value our opinions and preferences more than we value our brothers and sisters in Christ.

A Beautiful Conglomeration

We all come from so many different backgrounds and cultures. That is one of the things that I love most about the church. You would be hard pressed to gather together such a wide variety of people as what you see in the church. We come from the other side of the tracks, the suburbs and from upscale neighborhoods. The church is represented by every nation, race, color and language. It is a wonderful and beautiful conglomeration! But that doesn't come without its own set of problems. No one would feel totally comfortable worshipping among people with very different customs or traditions. That is why I have to constantly remind myself that the reason the Lord brings us together is not necessarily to meet our own needs, although that is important, but to serve Him and those of the church. This includes people very different from me; people for whom He died to demonstrate his love. Now, we have the opportunity to incarnate His grace by serving them.

Paul gives a good synopsis of all this in Galatians 5:13:

"You, my brothers and sisters, were called to be free. But do not use your freedom to indulge the flesh; rather, serve one another humbly in love."

We are completely free in Christ. There is no life more liberated than one that is in Christ. That being said, where do you find yourself? Has the Lord brought to mind what may be keeping you from loving that other follower of Christ who is so different from you? It may mean sacrifice on your part.

A True Life Example
There is a strained relationship in my life today. It all started with a preference of someone close to me that has placed a wedge between us. It is not a preference that I hold to and they feel so strongly over it that they consider me to be "in sin" because I refuse to agree with them.

At first, the disagreement was so strong that I held in feelings of resentment and found myself beginning to wrestle with bitterness. I began thinking, "Who is he to tell me how to handle this issue that is not addressed in the Bible?" I felt as though I was falsely accused and was labeled as sinful for nothing more than a preference. I felt that he had no right to invade my family with his convictions.

After several months, the Lord confronted me with these emotions and led me to go to him to seek reconciliation as far as he was able. Only he could decide whether this was an issue that would permanently divide us because it is an issue on which he stands so sternly. All I could do was to take responsibility for how I felt about his opinion of me.

I'm glad to say that we found some reconciliation. Both of us still believe our position to be the right one. I came to realize that he was mainly motivated out of a love and concern for me and my family. The question I had to wrestle with was whether or not I could love him enough to sacrifice my feelings of pride and if I could love him even if his opinion of me was that I was sinning against God.

We place so many obstacles in the way of loving one another. There may be preferences or opinions you are holding to that He may be wanting you to sacrifice for the sake of your brother or sister. Ultimately, there is no room for division or offences in the church over preferences. It is impossible to remain in the Vine and detach from the other branches. We will not completely agree with one another on every issue and we can't compromise the Bible in the least, but our main concern should always be for the sake of others when it comes to preferences. We may "win" the battle in a dispute with our brother or sister and lose them because of pride and an unwillingness to sacrifice our preferences. Or we can choose to give them preference by setting our own aside for their sake. By doing so, we can become grace incarnate in their eyes.

Chapter nine discussion questions.

1. Discuss some of the "gray issues" that you have seen in the church. What defines a gray issue – how do we know when the issue we're faced with truly is a gray issue?

2. Why do you think we get so passionate about our gray issues? What are we forgetting when we judge someone because they don't share our opinion about something that is not clearly defined in the Bible as something we must observe?

3. How serious to God is our judging of others concerning gray issues? What must we keep in mind as we are tempted to judge someone who doesn't share our opinion?

4. What was Paul's solution to keeping the balance regarding preferences? What are we saying to someone when we set aside our own preferences for their sake?

CHAPTER 10 - GRACE TO FORGIVE

Ephesians 4:32
"Be kind and compassionate to one another, forgiving each other, just as in Christ God forgave you."

He was literally left for dead. Pelted with stones, he collapsed and was carried outside the city by the Jews who had stoned him only to be dumped on the ground. The believers of the Lord Jesus, to whom he had preached, mournfully gathered around his body in amazement that he was taken from them so suddenly and violently. Their amazement would go through the roof as he opened his eyes, got to his feet and walked back into the city (Acts 14:19-20).

Unfortunately, this was not an isolated case for Paul. He explains to the Corinthians that five times he received thirty-nine lashes from the Jews (just one short of the 40 that they believed would kill a person), and endured the stoning we just spoke about (2 Corinthians 11:24-25). To say the least, Paul had suffered at the hands of his own countrymen. They hated the apostle with a passion and wanted nothing more than to be rid of him permanently. To them he was a deceiver and a traitor because he had left their faith to proclaim Jesus as the Messiah.

But what was Paul's opinion of his "would be" killers? Listen to his heart as he writes while sitting in a prison cell many years later - Romans 9:1-4A:

"I speak the truth in Christ—I am not lying, my conscience confirms it through the Holy Spirit—I have great sorrow and unceasing anguish in my heart. For I could wish that I myself were cursed and cut off from Christ for the sake of

---

my people, those of my own race, the people of Israel"

How could Paul have had this kind of love for these people-
enough love that he would wish he could bear their curse so that
they could be saved? In all the history of the church, there are few
who loved the Lord more deeply than Paul or were more
committed as a servant of Jesus. There are few who could claim
to have been used, to the extent he had, as a conduit of Christ's
love and truth to all he met and to millions of others since then.
Yet, Paul testifies that he would wish himself accursed, separated
from Christ who was his life, if only these people who were
responsible for so much suffering in his life would come to know
Him as their Savior. In essence he was saying that he would trade
his own salvation if they were to believe.

Paul went above and beyond to forgive those who
persecuted him. Of anyone, he should have reason to turn his back
on those who had turned their backs on him. He had every reason
to abandon his nation. Every reason, that is, but one: it was not
what his Lord had done.

As I think about some of the things that would pose an
obstacle to our relationship with God and one another, forgiveness
is an issue that rises to the top. For those who refuse to forgive
another, my prayer is that you might begin to experience healing
as you consider this issue of forgiveness in the context of grace. As
a believer in the Lord Jesus Christ, you have already experienced
the grace of forgiveness, having been on the receiving end. That is
where true, genuine forgiveness begins.

A Root of Bitterness

The problem that accompanies an unwillingness to forgive
someone who has wronged us is bitterness. Someone once said
that being bitter against someone else is like taking poison yourself
and waiting for the other person to die. The bitterness that results

is like a cancer that eats away at the soul of the person who is embittered. It can lead to our destruction mentally, emotionally and eventually, physically.

However, bitterness most often does not isolate itself, it tends to spread like a virus that is nearly impossible to contain. Bitterness, like misery, loves company. How many church splits have occurred because of bitterness that spread from one person to the next? So many relationships between believers and friends have been destroyed because one or both involved in an offense refuse to forgive. Listen to what the writer of the book of Hebrews said:

> "Make every effort to live in peace with everyone and to be holy; without holiness no one will see the Lord. See to it that no one falls short of the grace of God and that no bitter root grows up to cause trouble and defile many" (Hebrews 12:14-15).

Bitterness in the Greek is "pikria", metaphorically meaning a bitter root that produces bitter fruit or bitter hatred.[16] Whole families and churches can be consumed with bitterness that defiles them – a hatred that spreads from one member to another as they take on each other's offenses. To say the very least, bitterness "causes trouble." Once that root begins to grow it produces bitter fruit which is good for nothing.

By far the worst result of bitterness is the spiritual pollution it creates. Put bluntly, bitterness is sin, and it separates us from fellowship with other people and ultimately with God. John says:

> "Anyone who claims to be in the light but hates a brother or sister is still in the darkness. Anyone who loves their brother and sister lives in the light, and there is nothing in them to make them stumble. But anyone who hates a

brother or sister is in the darkness and walks around in the darkness. They do not know where they are going, because the darkness has blinded them." (1 John 2:9-11).

An unwillingness to forgive places us in darkness that blinds us from seeing clearly, disabling us spiritually. Hatred of a brother or sister takes us from the light and blinds us to God's work in our lives.

Blindness Caused by Bitterness

A number of years ago, Heather and I received a call from a college friend. We had lost touch with her, so we were pleasantly surprised when she called. She explained, however, that she and her husband were having some marital problems and needed someone to talk to, so we set a date to get together.

On the evening we met, we could tell right away from their demeanor that there were some deep problems. As we began to speak about their differences, he kept bringing up offenses his wife had committed against him. Honestly, they were very minor offenses having a lot to do with the effects of an illness she was experiencing rather than a character flaw. He went on and on about how she wouldn't keep up on her share of the household duties and some of the ways she was communicating that were offensive to him. Our friend was more than willing to work on the issues he mentioned, but when we suggested that he consider forgiving his wife, he took offense and wanted nothing more to do with us. Granted, our relationship was with her, but we were very careful not to suggest that he alone was to blame. He refused to forgive her, and we were saddened, but not shocked, when they divorced not long after.

This man was blind to his part in the conflict and the only thing he could see were his wife's offenses against him. He could not see his own responsibility for what was taking place in their relationship. He was in total darkness - blind to his own faults - and it was consuming him. That is what often happens to people who carry bitterness. Before long, the bitterness becomes a passion that seems to come up anytime the offender is mentioned in conversation. Generally speaking, those who are bitter believe themselves to be completely justified in their bitterness and attempt to get everyone they speak with to side with them against their offender.

I realize that there are some reading this with deep wounds, who have tragically been the victim of someone else's terrible sin. It could have happened years ago or just yesterday. It may have involved another believer or someone who does not know Christ. You cannot imagine ever forgiving the person who has hurt you – the wound is just too deep. As sincerely and tenderly as I can say this, you need to know that this, actually, is not about the person who hurt you. It is about you and your willingness to make the choice of forgiveness or the bitterness you will live with if you don't. It is actually about you and your relationship with God. It is about you trusting Him to do something in you that you can't possibly do yourself. It has to do with who you are in your identity with Christ!

The Choice is Yours

I want to go back to the Scripture that we read earlier from Hebrews 12 that speaks of the grace of God: "See to it that no one *falls short of the grace of God* and that no bitter root grows up to cause trouble and defile many..." (Hebrews 12:15, emphasis added). As a believer in the Lord Jesus, you have asked for and received His forgiveness. You have become the beneficiary of God's amazing grace. You understand the release from the bondage of your sin because you have accepted, by faith, God's forgiveness and now live in freedom. However, when you allow anger and bitterness toward someone to grow, you refuse to offer the release that has been freely given to you. Even though you enjoy the release and freedom given to you by God's grace, you refuse to offer it to someone else. You have come short of the grace of God. His grace must pass from the personal to the practical in our lives - in other words, we must not only receive His grace but also learn to extend it to others.

To God, it's a Big Deal

This is such an important issue to God. One of the most frightening scriptures I have ever read tells us that He will not grant forgiveness to those who will not forgive (Matthew 6:14-15). In other words, our relationship with God as our Father is compromised when we refuse to forgive someone else. He is still your Father, that will never change, but this sin places a barrier in your relationship with Him and it has deep implications for your life. Having forgiven us so much, He will not tolerate a heart that refuses to forgive. This is especially true when it comes to forgiving those who are fellow believers.

The reason this is so important to Him is because it reflects on His nature. He is the God who forgives and forgiveness is at the very heart of the gospel! God's forgiveness is unconditional, total and complete. By refusing to forgive, we distort and cheapen the gospel by placing conditions on it by our unwillingness to forgive. Those outside the faith examining our lives would have to wonder what the gospel could possibly offer them if they see that we hold bitterness toward one another.

Yet, it goes even deeper than that. You cannot grow in your relationship with Christ, and at the same time, hold bitterness in your heart. It is completely contrary to the character of Christ. He is, above all, first and foremost, One who forgives and we must incarnate His grace as those who are forgiven by forgiving others. As His people, there is no room for an unforgiving heart full of bitterness. We simply cannot abide in the Vine because the root of bitterness contaminates the branch.

But there is hope in what might seem like a hopeless situation. How can you find freedom from the prison of bitterness? Grace holds within itself the key to free you from that bondage. By grace, you do not face this mountain alone. Grace enables you to do what you can't do yourself!

Think of when you first trusted Christ. By His grace you came to Him when you understood your need for forgiveness, knowing that you had nothing to contribute to your own salvation. The same is true in finding freedom and release from bitterness or any other sin that entangles you. The power to overcome this obstacle comes through the enablement of the Holy Spirit within you! It is God's work in you, but you must acknowledge that you need Him and accept His grace, by faith, to move this mountain. By doing this, the obstacle is removed which is hindering the most important relationship you possess: your relationship with God!

By admitting to Him your inability to forgive, you open the way for grace to take over. You admit that holding on to bitterness is sin and you choose to let it go. Then, you trust Him to move you out of this prison cell you've been confined to. Our lives are a series of opportunities to trust Him to work in us and this is a huge step of faith for any who have the courage to take it. But perhaps the biggest step of faith which involves forgiveness is this: we must trust Him by giving to Him our right to get even.

To let go of the bitterness, we have to do so completely which includes letting go of the idea of getting even. Again, this is so hard to do depending on the nature of the offense. But, believe me, He will make it right. As our sovereign God, He knows every detail of our lives, even those in which we have been deeply hurt. He knows the pain you are feeling; He really does. If you will trust Him, He will use even this awful offense for your good and for the good of others. "Do not take revenge, my dear friends, but leave room for God's wrath, for it is written: 'It is mine to avenge; I will repay,' says the Lord" (Romans 12:19). We can completely trust Him to make it right and give Him the liberty to deal with the offender as He sees fit. When you are able to do this, it is no longer your battle but His. He will fight for you and you will be free!!

Forgiving Beyond Forgetting

Offenses are often impossible to forget. One look in the mirror was all it took to remind Paul of the pain he had endured at the hands of his own countrymen. He once said that he bore in his body the "marks of Jesus" (Galatians 6:17). I believe that some of those marks were the scars he received from beatings and the stoning he received at the hands of the Jews. He had not forgotten the things done to him but, by the immeasurable grace of God, he chose to forgive.

Of course, the greatest example is the One who forgave not only Paul, but you and me as well. I believe that one of the most striking sights in Heaven won't be the streets of gold or the splendor of the New Jerusalem. It will be the nail prints in the hands of the One who will stretch out His arms to welcome you there. Those nail prints will forever be a reminder of the Great Grace Giver, Jesus Himself, who forgave every offense you and I have ever committed against Him. Those nail prints will be an everlasting testimony of grace every time we see them. Your scars, whether seen or unseen, can be the same. If you allow them, they could become eternal reminders of God's grace to you.

Corrie's Choice

I'm sure many of you have read the book or seen the movie *The Hiding Place*. It is the true story of a family of believers in Holland during World War II that saved Jews from the Nazis by hiding them behind a false wall in their home until they were caught and sent to a concentration camp. Corrie ten Boom and her sister, Betsie, were sent to Ravensbruck where Betsie would later die.

What makes this story so powerful is the way it demonstrates how someone who endured so much horrific abuse could later offer forgiveness to one of her tormentors.

Corrie describes what it was like to meet one of her former guards:

"It was in a church in Munich that I saw him—a balding, heavyset man in a gray overcoat, a brown felt hat clutched between his hands. People were filing out of the basement room where I had just spoken, moving along the rows of wooden chairs to the door at the rear. It was 1947 and I had come from Holland to defeated Germany with the message that God forgives.

"It was the truth they needed most to hear in that bitter, bombed-out land, and I gave them my favorite mental picture. Maybe because the sea is never far from a Hollander's mind, I liked to think that that's where forgiven sins were thrown. 'When we confess our sins,' I said, 'God casts them into the deepest ocean, gone forever...'

"The solemn faces stared back at me, not quite daring to believe. There were never questions after a talk in Germany in 1947. People stood up in silence, in silence collected their wraps, in silence left the room.

"And that's when I saw him, working his way forward against the others. One moment I saw the overcoat and the brown hat; the next, a blue uniform and a visored cap with its skull and crossbones. It came back with a rush: the huge room with its harsh overhead lights; the pathetic pile of dresses and shoes in the center of the floor; the shame of walking naked past this man. I could see my sister's frail form ahead of me, ribs sharp beneath the parchment skin. Betsie, how thin you were!

"Now he was in front of me, hand thrust out: 'A fine message, Fräulein! How good it is to know that, as you say, all our sins are at the bottom of the sea!'

"And I, who had spoken so glibly of forgiveness, fumbled in my pocketbook rather than take that hand. He would not remember me, of course—how could he remember one prisoner among those thousands of women?

"But I remembered him and the leather crop swinging from his belt. I was face-to-face with one of my captors and my blood seemed to freeze.

"'You mentioned Ravensbruck in your talk,' he was saying, 'I was a guard there.' No, he did not remember me.

"'But since that time,' he went on, 'I have become a Christian. I know that God has forgiven me for the cruel things I did there, but I would like to hear it from your lips as well. Fräulein,' again the hand came out—'will you forgive me?'

"And I stood there—I whose sins had again and again to be forgiven—and could not forgive. Betsie had died in that place—could he erase her slow terrible death simply for the asking?

"It could not have been many seconds that he stood there—hand held out—but to me it seemed hours as I wrestled with the most difficult thing I had ever had to do.

"For I had to do it—I knew that. The message that God forgives has a prior condition: that we forgive those who have injured us. 'If you do not forgive men their trespasses,' Jesus says, 'neither will your Father in heaven forgive your trespasses.'

"I knew it not only as a commandment of God, but as a daily experience. Since the end of the war, I had had a home in Holland for victims of Nazi brutality. Those who were able to forgive their former enemies were also able to return to the outside world and rebuild their lives, no matter what the physical scars. Those who nursed their bitterness remained invalids. It was as simple and as horrible as that.

"And still I stood there with the coldness clutching my heart. But forgiveness is not an emotion—I knew that too. Forgiveness is an act of the will, and the will can function regardless of the temperature of the heart. '...Help!' I prayed silently. 'I can lift my hand. I can do that much. You supply the feeling.'

"And so woodenly, mechanically, I thrust my hand into the one stretched out to me. And as I did, an incredible thing took place. The current started in my shoulder, raced down my arm, sprang into our joined hands. And then this healing warmth seemed to flood my whole being, bringing tears to my eyes.

"'I forgive you, brother!' I cried. 'With all my heart!'

"For a long moment we grasped each other's hands, the former guard and the former prisoner. I had never known God's love so intensely, as I did then."[17]

As Corrie said, "Forgiveness is an act of the will..." It is a choice that we make,"...regardless of the temperature of the heart." She was able to forgive after praying for the help to do so and, in faith, stretched out her hand to one who treated her and her dear sister so brutally. God took over from there and Corrie, the former prisoner, was truly set free.

Just like you, I have often wondered why God allows us to go through such hardship and pain. He is a loving Father, yet He allows difficulties, offenses and even persecution into our lives.

Why is that? We will discuss this a little further in the next chapter, but I can't help but think it has something to do with this: it has been said that we cannot more closely reflect the character of God than when we forgive, than when we become the incarnation of grace. We are His children in a world which knows so little about forgiveness and so much about getting even. Maybe we shine brighter as a light to the world when they witness our willingness to forgive. Before their eyes, they see the gospel unfold. We become like our Savior and reflect His light to this terribly dark world. This brings to life the old adage in the most meaningful way – "to forgive is truly divine."

For you who are struggling with this issue of an unwillingness to forgive or bitterness, please take these first steps. You can do this by the Spirit's enablement. Having said that, you may also need to seek a Christian counselor or pastor, or at the very least, seek the prayers of those closest to you. Find the help that you need so that you can be free from this terrible set of shackles in your life created by bitterness or unforgiveness. You will never regret taking those first painful steps toward a sweet freedom you will enjoy the rest of your days!

Chapter ten discussion questions.
1. How might bitterness take control of a life, so much so that it blinds the one who harbors it?
2. What is the dominant characteristic of a person who holds unforgiveness or resentment against someone else? What do you notice about their conversations?
3. Grace holds the key to find release from the prison of bitterness. Grace steps into the situation when our ability to forgive is non-existent. Discuss our role needed for God to remove the mountain of bitterness from our lives.
4. How do we know, for sure, that we have been released from the prison of bitterness? What can you expect to find once God takes up your struggle for you?

CHAPTER 11 - GRACE FOR SUFFERING

1 Peter 5:10
"And the God of all grace, who called you to his eternal glory in Christ, after you have suffered a little while, will himself restore you and make you strong, firm and steadfast."

I was once in a Bible study when the topic of suffering came up. One of the participants in the study said that he believed there were things that happened to us to strengthen our faith and the rest was "just life." I don't believe that at all! Our God is sovereign and nothing that happens to us is a result of chance, accident or "just life." Granted, everyone suffers whether you know the Lord or not, but for the believer, there is always a reason for what we experience, and grace is given as we face those circumstances if we choose to receive it.

I can testify that during times of suffering in my own life, I have looked more for relief than for the grace to handle the suffering. That is the typical response when we're hurting, whether it be physical, emotional or psychological. When it hurts, we want immediate relief. How interesting it is that the Lord, more often than not, chooses to bring us through the suffering rather than stopping it altogether. As He told Paul who suffered from a "thorn in the flesh," an ailment we are told little about, "My grace is sufficient for you, for my power is made perfect in weakness" (2 Corinthians 12:9).

Why, God, do We Suffer?

Why would God, as a loving Father, allow us to experience suffering? It seems some people have to endure suffering all through their lives while others seem to have an occasional brush with it. Then there are entire nations or races of people who have experienced suffering under dictatorships, slavery, war and disease. Our world is full of suffering and pain.

All of us have our own set of burdens. We find ourselves faced with terrible circumstances and have no idea of how to handle or even begin to imagine how we will ever get through them. At some point we will all lose someone – a spouse, child, parent or friend. Anyone who has experienced this kind of loss wonders how to go on without our loved one. I think the most difficult suffering comes from the empty feeling after such a loss. It may lead us to think our life is unbearable, but we can find comfort in knowing that Jesus fully understands the pain that accompanies death.

The death of Lazarus brought tears to Jesus (John 11:33-36). He knew He would raise Lazarus from the dead, yet He wept at Lazarus' death. I believe His tears displayed to all that He shared in the pain of Lazarus' sisters, Martha and Mary, and everyone else who was mourning him. I think those tears show that, even to this day, His heart is broken over our loss as well. He shares in our pain! He took on human flesh, in part, to know from experience our human condition. That is the reason we can also know, with certainty, that His grace will bear us through our times of great loss. He knows our pain. As broken as we are, and the more broken we become, the more grace we will receive because His power is perfected in weakness.

When we suffer, we feel we need to understand and have the right for an explanation. But the truth is, as much as we would like to know the reason for our suffering, God may not be willing to reveal His purposes to us anytime soon, if ever at all. This is hard to hear, especially if you're the kind of person who attempts to find a reason for every event in your life. You must remember that this suffering is His prerogative. He, as the Sovereign Creator of the universe, knows what He is doing, even when it makes no sense to us at all. His question to us is, "Will you trust Me through all the pain and uncertainty?"

Even though we may not have an answer for what we're going through, what I can say is the Bible does give us some understanding and, I pray, some peace in the midst of all the chaos. Not all of our questions will be answered, but we can be sure that He has a reason for our trials.

Self-Inflicted Suffering

It is so important to note that some of the suffering we experience we bring upon ourselves. When we sin, there will be consequences. Peter spoke about this in 1 Peter 4:15: "If you suffer, it should not be as a murderer or thief or any other kind of criminal, or even as a meddler." As you look at the suffering you may be enduring, ask yourself these questions: "Have I made poor decisions which have brought on this pain? Am I confident I am in God's will as I have made these choices? Have I gotten ahead of God by being impatient and pushing ahead without knowing His will or timing?"

I have personally experienced suffering in my own life because I was impatient and would not wait on God to provide His answer to my circumstances. And, I have spoken to some Christians who were open about their sin, yet surprised that God would allow suffering in their lives. We can avoid unnecessary suffering simply by examining ourselves in light of God's word. If we know we have sinned and are suffering because of the consequences, we must confess the sin to Him and turn away from it by applying the principles of sanctification we spoke about earlier in the book (chapters 4-6). However, it is possible that our motives may not be pure and we are not even aware of it. I find that I can often justify many of my actions regardless of whether or not these choices reflect *His* best for me. That is why we must weigh our decisions against His word because the Bible "judges the thoughts and attitudes of the heart" (Hebrews 4:12).

An important positive result for us to understand is that suffering produces growth. As I look back over the times of suffering in my life, I see that I have learned a lot more through the valley experiences than I have on the mountain top. Suffering has a solidifying effect upon us. Those things we learn in the valley generally remain with us for a lifetime.

Grace on Tap

For the most part, suffering has a way of depleting our own resources and making us weak within ourselves. This is when God's grace can illuminate our path. When Paul asked to be released from his suffering, the response he got is that God's grace "is sufficient for you" (2 Corinthians 12:9). To be honest, that doesn't settle well with me. I see myself, for the most part, as a strong individual. But there have been times when that strength was so depleted that I had nowhere else to turn. That is when the miracle of His grace emerges. Where our strength leaves off is where His grace begins! As a child of God, you have the opportunity to experience the grace of God poured into your life in the midst of your suffering. This grace enables and empowers you to bear up under the pain and to come through to the other side. We must remember that the mystery of grace in suffering is that it comes to us when we have come to the end of ourselves! That seems to be a common prerequisite for grace to be received.

Without getting into too much detail, Heather and I endured a very painful period in our lives. It took place at the end of nearly five years of missions work in the Eastern European country of Estonia. Before we arrived, I thought missions would be the most rewarding and satisfying work imaginable. Reality hit shortly after our arrival when language training began. It was a struggle, especially for me.

After a lot of blood, sweat and tears, along with a heavy dose of grace, the language skills improved and I was able to teach the Bible without the help of an interpreter. We were making several friends and feeling more at home in this foreign land. We had even seen several children come to faith in Christ and many of our friends were showing genuine interest in the Bible and spiritual things.

On a personal note, we had been married for about 10 years and still did not have children. One of our friends directed us to a local doctor who could run some tests to find out the reason for our infertility. We went through a series of tests but were not very optimistic of getting any answers.

At about that same time and out of nowhere, we received a letter from the American consulate in Tallinn informing us that we may have to leave the country. In an effort to eliminate certain foreign residents, the Estonian government was tightening requirements by disallowing tourist visas. Up until that time, we could exit the country for a day and would then be eligible to return and remain for a three month period. We had previously attempted to receive a business visa but were denied. The consulate informed us that the tourist visas would probably end and we should start making arrangements to leave.

This was a huge struggle for us both, but especially for me. I couldn't imagine that God would actually want us out of Estonia. I wrestled with Him every day in prayer, pleading with Him to allow us to stay. How could we leave when opportunities were beginning to open to us? How could He possibly want us to abandon the kids we had led to Him? Surely, He would provide a way for us to stay.

On another one of those fateful mornings, we received a phone call from the consulate who told us that a certain Estonian doctor, who had done some tests, was needing to get ahold of us right away. As I said, we were not very optimistic when we left the doctor and even though they had our names, they apparently had lost our phone number. They did know that we were

Americans which was why they contacted the consulate.

I called the doctor and was completely stunned by hearing that the tests he had done on us revealed that Heather had cancer. He told me he was fairly certain of the results and that she should get back to America immediately because he didn't have the equipment in Estonia to treat her. Within a few short days, she flew to Miami, Florida, where her dad lived at the time. Our fears of cancer were realized and she had surgery less than a week after arriving in Miami.

Meanwhile, I was still in Estonia wrapping everything up because when she flew back to the States, we didn't know for certain that it was cancer. Those were the hardest days of our lives. Within a couple of months, we had lost what I felt was the dream of a lifetime as well as our hope of having biological children. It was devastating. I remember packing boxes until late into the night and saying goodbye to shocked and overwhelmed friends.

But, by the time I boarded the plane for America, my struggle with God was over. Both of us were broken people which made us the perfect candidates for grace. I can't begin to tell you how He has used that suffering in our lives. We don't have all the answers to questions as to why those things happened, but we are able to rest much easier today in His sovereignty and grace.

We received grace because we knew we needed it. However, grace is something that can be refused or resisted. Think about it; grace is always available, but only if received willingly and in humility. Take, for example, grace given for salvation, "For it is by grace you have been saved, through faith— and this is not from yourselves, it is the gift of God" (Ephesians 2:8). Just as an unbeliever can refuse the gift of the grace of God for salvation, so we can refuse the gift of His grace to bear us through our times of suffering.

I wonder if that were the case with Paul. Before his encounter with Jesus, he was a self-confident, self-sustained

Pharisee. I'm sure there were weaknesses he wrestled with throughout his life, but when I think of Paul, I think of a strong person who charged ahead without looking back. Three times he asked the Lord to remove the thorn without any result. He may have attempted to overcome the thorn in his own strength. Perhaps it wasn't until he surrendered his struggle that he finally found that grace would flow into his life.

We want to solve our own problems; we want to work it out ourselves. Yet, until we yield to the Lord Jesus' power in our lives, the grace may not flow. "Let us then approach God's throne of grace with confidence, so that we may receive mercy and find grace to help us in our time of need" (Hebrews 4:16). The confidence we have to draw near to His throne is a confidence we have in Him, not ourselves. We come to Him for the mercy and grace we need, not to show Him how wonderfully strong, capable and equipped we are to handle our own struggles. I wonder how much suffering we endure needlessly because we refuse to let go of the struggle and approach the throne to accept the grace we so desperately need. To remain in the Vine, we will need to admit that the Vine is our sole source of grace and that reliance upon our own strength is actually a refusal to accept His. You cannot remain in the Vine if pride hinders you from accepting His gift of grace.

Our Suffering Can Help Others

Suffering leaves its scars; it is painful, but at the same time, very powerful. When suffering is so intense that you are tempted to move beyond it at all costs, it is important for you to realize that, if you are willing, your journey can have an eternal effect on others! Suffering has a way of isolating us, making us think that we are the only one who understands our painful circumstances. We who have already suffered must provide hope and comfort for those now having to traverse that same or similar lonely experience. It is our responsibility to one another to encourage each other so that no one has to feel he or she is walking alone. Paul encourages the Corinthian church to have this mindset when he says,

> "Praise be to the God and Father of our Lord Jesus Christ, the Father of compassion and the God of all comfort, who comforts us in all our troubles, so that we can comfort those in any trouble with the comfort we ourselves receive from God" (2 Corinthians 1:3-4).

This is perhaps one of the most precious gifts we have the privilege of giving one another. Our God of all comfort is willing to partner with us to help others through the most difficult times of their lives. How would it feel to see God using you to come alongside someone who is going through the same suffering you had to endure and offer them the help that He gave to you? You can become grace incarnate to someone who right now is broken to pieces.

In our day, there are circumstances that carry with them such a shameful stigma that those who experience them may seem, in their own minds, to be wounded beyond recovery. Divorce and abortion are examples that occur so often. Sexual assault and addiction are all around us, even in the church. The pain that is experienced through these things can last a lifetime. Shame may keep these secrets locked away in the dark. However, if you have experienced this pain, consider that someone may benefit when you speak up about your own suffering. You need not share all the painful details in order to share the grace and comfort that God provides to endure such difficult trials, but you should share them with those who need to hear it.

Perhaps the person who needs that comfort is as close to you as your own child. As a parent, God may call you to be vulnerable enough with your children in order to save them from making avoidable mistakes or showing them that you understand if they already have. You may be the person God has in mind to help them in their healing as you point them to the Savior who carried you through and gave you the comfort you needed! You can become the reflection of one of the most precious facets of God by your incarnation of grace.

Suffering Strengthens Faith

Suffering also strengthens our faith. While addressing believers who were suffering and were about to suffer even more under the evil Roman Emperor Nero, Peter instructs the believers to,

> "...greatly rejoice, though now for a little while you may have had to suffer grief in all kinds of trials. These have come so that the proven genuineness of your faith—of greater worth than gold, which perishes even though refined by fire—may result in praise, glory and honor when Jesus Christ is revealed" (1 Peter 1:6-7).

Just as fire refines gold, so suffering refines our faith. In other words, there are things in our lives that have a way of corroding our faith. There is sin that gets in the way of a genuine relationship with the Savior. There are habits, distractions and addictions that draw us away from Him. There may even be idols, such as financial security or prestige that blind us to Him. Good things like work and ambition can replace Him. Suffering has the effect of bringing us back to the basics while re-aligning and re-prioritizing the things that really matter in life. We may need to be unencumbered by our own ambition and desires in order to see more clearly God's best for our lives!

Removing the "dross" only comes when the heat is applied. Our trial by fire is an opportunity given to us by our sovereign

God, who makes no mistakes, to purify and strengthen our faith. There are apparently certain things we can only learn through the fire, as painful as that may be. I can honestly say that I have never sought after God as eagerly as in those times of trial. Then, after having passed through, I have found my faith strengthened as I venture beyond the suffering to enjoy a deeper level of intimacy, praise and worship in my relationship with Jesus.

Notice what he says about our refined faith; it is "of greater worth than gold" which perishes, but may be found to God's "praise, glory and honor" when the Lord Jesus returns. Once we get through this life and arrive home, we will look back at our times of trial and think of how glad we were to have endured them. We will praise Him for what he has done, how He strengthened us and gave us the grace to overcome. Our faith, having been tried by fire, will shine to His praise, glory and honor. All who know us will marvel at what God has done in our lives as we trusted Him through the fire (Romans 8:18).

Heather and I left Estonia and returned there only for a short trip a few months later to properly say goodbye to our friends. We still don't have all the answers for the suffering we went through but saw our faith refined in the end. I realized sometime later that my identity is not as a Christian or as a missionary or as an American, but is found in Christ. That one fact has changed my life completely and had a lot to do with the writing of this book.

Allow the Suffering, Resist the Anger

There is a real danger that if we fail to trust Him through the suffering, we may become angry and bitter. If you begin to doubt that He is good and that He has the best in mind for you, your suffering may turn you inward. Trusting in His sovereignty means that you believe He has only the best in mind for you even though it is extremely painful (Job 13:15). It may be that there will be times in your life that you will have to go through the breaking process – breaking that you know has come from Him. But, once you have been broken by His hand, you realize that He is the only One who can put your life back together again. You come to an end of your own resources and reach, as a child, in the only direction you are able – toward the arms of your Father.

Heather has since recovered from her cancer for which we are eternally grateful. God has, since then, also blessed us with our adopted son, Benjamin. He is such a blessing and a testimony of God's great grace in our lives and answer to many years of prayer by us, our families and friends.

> "All this is for your benefit, so that the grace that is reaching more and more people may cause thanksgiving to overflow to the glory of God. ... For our light and momentary troubles are achieving for us an eternal glory that far outweighs them all (2 Corinthians 4:15, 17).

> "I consider that our present sufferings are not worth comparing with the glory that will be revealed in us" (Romans 8:18).

Think of your current suffering as one day bringing glory to God! Should we choose to respond to it in faith, trusting Him for the results, great glory shall be given to Him and we will be completely amazed at His marvelous work in our lives! At that time, all the pieces will fit together and we will see how He used even our suffering for His glory and for our good.

Chapter eleven discussion questions.

1. Discuss how Jesus' power is perfected in weakness. What does that say about how we should approach our suffering from the time we enter into it? What makes this approach so difficult?

2. Would you agree with the statement that grace can be refused or resisted? Why would you think the Lord would withhold grace before we respond to Him out of our weakness?

3. Think of the suffering you have endured in your life. How might these experiences help someone else? Who might that person be?

4. Our suffering may have the effect of bringing "praise, glory and honor" to Jesus when He returns. Discuss how a refined faith, tested by fire through trials, can have that result.

CHAPTER 12 - HOME – THE PLACE OF FREEDOM

Galatians5:13
"You, my brothers and sisters, were called to be free. But do not use your freedom to indulge the flesh; rather, serve one another humbly in love."

One of my earliest memories of something that was really historically significant in my lifetime was the return of U.S. servicemen who were released after having been prisoners of war in Vietnam. I remember watching these men on the news, some very gaunt and frail, getting off planes and being completely swarmed by those who loved them. Whole families of wives and children, parents and siblings would stampede to gather these men, most of whom were sobbing, in their arms with no intent of letting go now that they had them back.

Some of those servicemen took a moment to kneel down on the tarmac and kiss their home soil. Even as a boy, I wondered what they had been through. Most returned home with stories of torture and mistreatment in prison camps that were infested with roaches and rats. They were tortured beyond belief and most would carry physical and psychological wounds for the rest of their lives.

Imagine what it would have been to face torturers day after day, some for several years, dreading what each new day would bring. Think of the pain they endured during long hours of interrogations through which they were beaten or made to stand on stacked stools for days or kneel on gravel for hours on end.[18] Think of the dread of imagining what was coming next. Many had little hope of ever leaving those camps alive.

Then finally, after so many years, after so many beatings and abuse and uncertainty, the day came for them to leave their tormentors. They were cleaned up and flown home to be greeted by their families. The moment that I witnessed on television was the fulfillment of what they had only dreamt of through all those years of agony; the dream of finally realizing, "I'm home."

What a sense of freedom these men must have enjoyed! They could go where they pleased, eat what they liked, hold those who were dear to them or just sit to listen to their voices. Freedom was probably never so sweet as it was in those first few days after gaining their liberty. They were finally home which is where freedom is best experienced.

Are You Home Yet?

Many Christians today have yet to come home. There is a freedom that we were born into when we were born again which has the power to change our spiritual lives if understood and applied by faith. We can live in the reality of home, the place of security and rest, when we begin to understand and apply by faith the truths we find in the Bible, some of which we have discussed through these chapters. The reverse is also true. We may also choose to live apart from the freedom which is ours in Christ simply by ignoring the truths that set us free. In other words, we can choose to live our lives apart from God's promises and remain as if we are still prisoners.

There is a reality to the bondage we may choose to follow. For some, it is a bondage to the way things have always been done. The status quo is never questioned nor is there consideration that there could be some other way to live. For others, the idea of living a life in the reality of grace is simply too risky. It is safer to stay put than to venture beyond the border of rules which others have established for them to live by.

To be sure, a life of grace is a life of risk. This risk doesn't come in the form of "falling into sin." Some of the worst moral failures I have witnessed among Christians have occurred in believers who came from the strictest religious traditions. Those who have a true appreciation of grace are less likely to fall into sin because their motivation for holiness doesn't come from a set of rules. The risk, or a better word may be "adventure," comes in the wonder of what God may do in your life now that you are free. It is not a freedom to do as you please. It is a freedom to live for Him, to risk everything you are and have, to live for His glory. It is an unwillingness to settle for anything less than His very best for your life.

Through the course of this book, we have looked at different ways we, as followers of Christ, choose to live our lives. Personally, I have walked down both paths. After becoming a believer, I attempted to live under self-induced expectations of myself or the expectations of others, rather than Christ's expectations of me, which led to a lot of disappointment. I have also been given the opportunity of believing God's word and allowing Jesus to live His life through me by faith which marked the beginning of my adventure. It is a life of incarnating grace.

I wanted to wrap up this book by looking at these contrasting ways of living and the freedom that can be experienced if we choose to live by incarnating grace. Even before we reach our heavenly home, we can even now begin to experience the freedom in Christ which overcomes the power of sin, legalism, bitterness, our frailties and the dominance of self.

Freedom in Christ

Any freedom we may enjoy in Christ can be compromised by our sinful nature. The enemy, who would never want us to enjoy any freedom, will offer to us a "fitting" substitute if we are willing to accept it. Or, we may choose the freedom of home, the best place freedom can be enjoyed.

In Christ, I am free from the power of sin...to live free of guilt and shame (Romans 6:7).

Sin causes separation from God. Even after we are saved, sin causes a divide between us and God leading to an estrangement of that precious relationship. The result is a stagnation in our spiritual lives. When we hold on to some sin we are faced with the resulting effects of guilt and shame because we know that is not how we are to live. God's Spirit will not allow us the liberty to live in sin, He will always convict us when we make the choice to knowingly sin.

Guilt and shame are dreadful tormentors. Guilt places us under the magnifying glass and exposes the sin we struggle with while pointing its bony finger into our chest until we are left completely exposed, with nothing to say. Guilt leaves us with a complete sense of failure and an impotence to do anything about it. Shame pulls us even further away from God. It attacks our very person; telling us we are worthless and beyond hope. It keeps us from allowing anyone in to witness our struggle. Shame has no companion and wants to keep its victim in complete isolation. It whispers that it would be too shameful to expose our inner selves and invite others to share in the struggle. Above all, shame wants absolutely nothing to do with God.

"Home" in this instance is knowing, by faith, that we are free from the power of sin. It is taking God at His word (which basically is the definition of faith) and giving it the freedom to take root in our lives. Remember, we are to allow the truth of the word of God to dictate our experience, not allow experience to dictate the truth of God's word. I know firsthand that this is really hard to do when your sin looms large! However, He has said that those who are in Christ are free from the power of sin. God is the only One who has the audacity to say such a thing, but also has all the credentials to back it up. He is also the only One who can make this freedom possible through the work of His Spirit.

If shame and guilt are the tormentors of sin, they are replaced by two welcome friends – joy and peace. Once you have confessed your sin to Him and turned from it, you can place your faith in the FACT, according to Romans 6, that you are dead to the power of sin. Then, consider what your life will be now that you are dead to it and offer your body to God as a living sacrifice. This frees you to enjoy the relationship which the Father desires to have with you. These two friends, joy and peace, are gifts that He brings into the relationship and are mentioned, along with love, as the first three blessings of the fruit of the Spirit (Galatians 5:22).

In Christ, I am free from the power of legalism...to serve God and others with the pure motivation of love.

Legalism is a very heavy burden to bear. It places servants of God under obligation to the law by placing a yoke around their necks they can never lift. It prods those under that yoke to work harder and harder to do more or risk losing the favor of God and man. It is relentless and unwilling to allow any to rest. Those under its influence live under fear of disappointment and guilt should they fail. Yet, failure is a constant reality because no human, outside of Jesus, has ever been able to live in complete obedience to the law, nor were we intended to.

The purpose of the law is to shine light on Christ as the One who could save us when we place our faith in Him because He is the fulfillment of the law (Galatians 3:23-26). And, as the fulfillment of the law, He is the only One who can release us from it.

There are those who would place believers in Jesus back under the law once they were saved from it. Some do this to gather a following. Others see it as a means of controlling those who are under their sphere of influence. Many simply lead others to strict obedience to the law without understanding there could be a better way. Regardless of the motive, Paul fought against this with all his might which was the very reason he wrote the book of Galatians. He wanted these new believers to be delivered from those who would place them back under the law (Galatians 3:10-29).

Anyone who has been released from legalism no longer serves God and others out of fear of failing but from a different motivation: they serve out of love. Being released from the harsh bondage of legalism has that effect. The prisoner set free is completely transformed by the love of Jesus who set him free so that he can genuinely love his Savior in return. It is from that source of love that service to Him naturally flows.

The danger of legalism is always present. It can take many forms today when an opinion about something not directly addressed in the Bible becomes a conviction and, before long, emerges as a doctrine that must be obeyed by all. We must be careful not to allow our own or someone else's opinion to take us away the freedom we have in Christ. As Paul wrote to the Galatians, "It is for freedom that Christ has set us free; therefore, keep standing firm and do not be subject again to a yoke of slavery" (Galatians 5:1).

In Christ I am free from the power of bitterness...to live without the chains of anger and hatred.

True forgiveness occurs when we first understand and appropriate God's forgiveness of us through the gospel. If I can see how He has forgiven me, I can begin to understand how I can truly forgive another. But, if I refuse to forgive, I will be dealing with the effects of bitterness for the rest of my life. I will not grow in my relationship with God because the source from which I am receiving life is not the "Vine of Christ" but the "root of bitterness."

There are many followers of Christ who live from the wrong life source. Many Christians today are scarred with anger toward people, some who are no longer in their lives or may have even died. No matter who our anger is directed toward, Jesus is waiting for those who struggle with this burden to surrender it to Him. Remember, this is not about the offender, it is about you and your willingness to hand it over to your Savior.

If you would, once and for all, decide to give Him the bitterness that you were never meant to carry, He would remove the chains of anger and hatred that weigh you down. "Home" for someone in this struggle is resting your faith in His ability to do the impossible – for you to be released from your bitterness to find true freedom. It means standing firm in your faith each time the offender is brought to mind. It means trusting God to make it right, even if the offender seems to have escaped justice. We can know that we have Someone who stands beside us, pouring grace into our lives if we would only trust Him. We can find freedom by trusting Him to do what we can't do ourselves – trust Him for the incarnation of the grace to forgive.

In Christ I am free from my own frailty...to live in the reality of grace when faced with suffering.

So many experiencing suffering can't see how it could ever produce anything that could be of any value or benefit. The pain generally blinds us from seeing anything other than the suffering. But, in the suffering is an opportunity to receive the beautiful pearl of the grace of God. As you know, a pearl is formed from the irritation of sand within the clam. The irritation of suffering produces a need within us that only God can meet. He gives grace that has the potential to change us completely even though the suffering may not end. It can be of great value if we allow it.

When we come to the end of our own abilities and acknowledge our inability to deal with the source of our suffering, we will receive the grace to stand up under it. Strange as it may seem, our weaknesses actually becomes our greatest strength. Jesus told this to Paul as he suffered: "My grace is sufficient for you, for my power is made perfect in weakness" (2 Corinthians 12:9). Broken people are the perfect candidates to receive God's grace. His grace may not come with a restored relationship or immediate physical healing. It may not come in the way we would hope or imagine, but it will come just the way He has designed and there could be no greater way than that!

"Home" for someone in this situation is being willing to allow Him the freedom to work out His strength in you as He chooses. Then, you can say along with Paul, "Therefore I will boast all the more gladly about my weaknesses, so that Christ's power may rest on me" (2 Corinthians 12:9b). We can trust Him to work out His power in us as we yield to Him our resources and efforts in dealing with our suffering. And, never forget this, He loves you with all His heart. He knows what you're going through and is ready to give you all the grace you need!

In Christ, I am free from the power of self...to live to serve God and others.

It is what I invest into you that will last into eternity. A look at the life of Jesus is to see a life spent for others. As God incarnate, He came not to be served, but to serve (Mark 10:45). Jesus shared His life-giving power one life at a time, day after day, from one person to the next. He touched thousands of lives with healing; physically, emotionally and especially, spiritually. His purpose was to invest Himself into others and was the perfect example as God's incarnation of grace. The thing is, He is still doing that today. He is now grace incarnate through you and me.

To live for Jesus, or rather, to allow Him to live His life through you, is to live so much bigger than yourself! We all have the potential to impact this world in ways that we can't begin to imagine. Those who choose to "remain in the Vine" willingly invest into the lives of others. That is part of the fruit that is born. The fear of others fades away; the fear of failure diminishes. The ever-present power of self – self-consumption, self-indulgence, self-pity, self-interest, all that turns us inward – is replaced with an outflow of love and concern for God and for others. Fruit begins to ripen.

We begin to see the world through different eyes. Instead of the dread of what lies ahead, there is the expectation of wonderful things to come. We are free to live the life He designed for us when we trust in His sovereign leading in our lives. We can be sure that He will care for us as His children. I believe that is the very essence of what the Christian life is to be. It is not a set of rules to be followed but a trusting, living, breathing relationship with God through His Spirit. It is a life of freedom, "Now the Lord is the Spirit, and where the Spirit of the Lord is, there is freedom" (2 Corinthians 3:17).

I pray that you have found some degree of freedom in these pages. The Christian life is not a life of impossibility, but of endless possibilities once He is given His rightful place! Your willingness to allow His Spirit to live the life of Jesus, grace incarnate, through you will open possibilities you never could have imagined. May He bless you as you step forward into those great possibilities that lie ahead!!! Your adventure begins as you become the incarnation of His grace.

Chapter twelve discussion questions.

1. What comes to mind as you consider a freedom that is yours in Christ that has been taken away as a captive?
2. The freedom we enjoy is founded on what God has said in His word. What keeps us from trusting what He has said in order to receive freedom?
3. Discuss the paradox that our freedom is found in our surrender to God rather than our fighting for it. Why do we so often struggle rather than yield?
4. What are the first steps you will take as your adventure begins?

NOTES

1.   Taken from *Charles F. Stanley Study Bible* by Charles F. Stanley Copyright ©2009 by Charles F. Stanley. Used by permission of Thomas Nelson. www.thomasnelson.com

2.   Matt Williams, The Prodigal Son's Father Shouldn't Have Run! (Biola Magazine, Web. Summer 2010). Used by permission.

3.   Earley, Pete. "CIA Traitor Aldrich Ames" (Crime Library, Criminal Minds and Methods. N.p., n.d. Web. 12 Dec. 2014). Used by permission.

4.   Taken from *Vine's Complete Expository Dictionary of Old and New Testament Words* by W.E. Vine, Merrill F. Unger, William White, Jr. Copyright © 1985 by W.E. Vine, Merrill F. Unger, William White, Jr. Used by permission of Thomas Nelson. www.thomasnelson.com

5.   Bond-servant, *Thayer's Greek Lexicon of the New Testament*, by Joseph Thayer, Hendrickson Publishers, Peabody, Massachusetts. Used by permission. All rights reserved.

6.   Count, *Thayer's Greek-English Lexicon of the New Testament*, by Joseph H. Thayer, (Hendrickson Publishers, Peabody, Massachusetts. Used by permission. All rights reserved.

7.   Me-me /i/12-hrs-everybody-has-their-own-opinions-on-drug-and-13464238, May 1, 2017

8.   Taken from *Vines Complete Expository Dictionary of Old and New Testament Words* by W.E. Vine, Merrill F. Unger, William White, Jr. Copyright © 1985 by W.E. Vine, Merrill F. Unger, William White, Jr. Used by permission of Thomas Nelson. www.thomasnelson.com

9.   U.S. Department of Agriculture, Forest Service, (How Aspens Grow), Public Domain, https://www.fs.fed.us/wildflowers/beauty/aspen/grow.shtml

10. Taken from *Believer's Bible Commentary, New Testament* by William MacDonald Copyright © 1989 by William MacDonald. Used by permission of Thomas Nelson. www.thomasnelson.com

11. The Root of the Righteous by Aiden Wilson Tozer, Moody Publications, 2015. Used by permission.

12. Taken from Believer's Bible Commentary, New Testament by William MacDonald Copyright ©1989 by William MacDonald. Used by permission of Thomas Nelson. www.thomasnelson.com

13. Gidget Fuentes, Honor the Fallen, (Military Times, Web, November 10, 2006). (https://thefallen.militarytimes.com/marine-cpl-jason-l-dunham/257227) Used by permission.

14. Final Report on the Capsizing on 28 September 1994 in the Baltic Sea of the RO-RO Passenger Vessel MV Estonia; the Joint Accident Investigation on Commission of Estonia, Finland and Sweden, December 1997, Estonia, Public Domain.

15. Rebecca Manley Pippert, Out of the Salt Shaker into the World, Intervarsity Press, 1979. Used by permission, Fair Use.

16. Taken from Vine's Complete Expository Dictionary of Old and New Testament Words by W.E. Vine, Merrill F. Unger, William White, Jr. Copyright © 1985 by W.E. Vine, Merrill F. Unger, William White, Jr. Used by permission of Thomas Nelson. www.thomasnelson.com

17. Corrie ten Boom, with Jamie Buckingham, Tramp for the Lord (Jove Books, The Berkley Publishing Group, New York, 1974). Used by permission - Corrie ten Boom Fonds.

18. Maureen Callhan, Tortured in Notorious 'Hanoi Hilton', 11 GIs were Unbreakable (New York Post, Maureen Callhan, Feb. 15, 2014). Used by permission.

www.ingramcontent.com/pod-product-compliance
Lightning Source LLC
Chambersburg PA
CBHW071000040426
42443CB00007B/596